The Rainbow After the Storm

Surviving and Thriving After a Cancer Diagnosis

Joann Abrahamsen

www.joannabrahamsen.com

The Rainbow After the Storm

Surviving and Thriving After a Cancer Diagnosis

By Joann Abrahamsen

First Printing: July, 2026

ISBN: 979-8-9866531-3-6

Published by:
Change Your Life Press
9 The Crossway
Yonkers, NY 10701
(914) 476-8131

www.joannabrahamsen.com

Permission granted to reprint the "Self-Hypnosis Suggestion" as outlined in the NGH Certification Training with credit to Dr. Richard Harte and the National Guild of Hypnotists: www.NGH.net

Joann Abrahamsen is available to speak at your business or conference event on a variety of topics. Go to her website www.joannabrahamsen.com, or send her an email joann4@optonline.net , or call her at (914) 476-8131.

Joann Abrahamsen
Hypnosis For a Change
9 The Crossway
Yonkers, NY 10701
914-476-8131

www.joannabrahamsen.com

Go to my website www.joannabrahamsen.com and click on the offer *Reprogram Your Subconscious Mind.* You will then be on my mailing list, and you will be notified of future books.

If you would like to discuss your goals with me and book a no obligation 15-minute online session, send me an email at joann4@optonline.net and put in the subject line: Zoom consultation screening. Include in the body of the email what your challenge is.

Joann Abrahamsen is available to speak at your business or conference event on a variety of topics. Go to her website www.joannabrahamsen.com for a list of topics and send her an email to discuss booking her:

joann4@optonline.net.

Dedication

This book is lovingly dedicated to every person whose life has been touched by cancer—those who are newly diagnosed, those currently in treatment, those living beyond cancer, and the family members and caregivers who walk beside them with unwavering love and support.

I am especially grateful to the courageous cancer survivors who generously entrusted me with their personal stories. Although most of the names in this book have been changed to protect their privacy, the experiences, emotions, and lessons they shared are real. Thank you for allowing me to tell your stories. My hope is that your words will offer comfort, courage, and hope to others who are traveling a similar path.

May every reader discover that even after life's darkest storms, there is always the possibility of hope... and the promise of a rainbow.

This book is also dedicated with deep appreciation to the entire cancer care team at New York-Presbyterian Westchester (Lawrence Hospital).

From the moment of my diagnosis through surgery, chemotherapy, radiation, follow-up care, and survivorship, you walked beside me with kindness, expertise, and compassion. Every physician, nurse, technician, therapist, receptionist, and staff member played an important role in my journey.

Thank you for the care you provide, the comfort you offer, and the hope you give to every patient who walks through your doors.

To My Husband, Robert

There are no words that can fully express my gratitude for everything you have been throughout my cancer journey.

From the day I heard the words, "You have cancer," you never left my side. You sat beside me in doctors' offices, took careful notes, asked questions I never would have thought to ask, and remembered the details when my mind was too overwhelmed to do so.

You learned lymphatic massage so you could help me manage my lymphedema. Night after night, you patiently helped me put on my lymphedema garment, offering not only your hands but also your encouragement as I learned to accept the permanent changes cancer brought into my life.

As a skilled hypnotist, you guided me through hypnosis sessions that eased my fear, reduced the side effects of chemotherapy and radiation, and reminded me that even during the most difficult days, my mind could become a source of comfort and strength.

You never tried to take away my fears. Instead, you helped me face them with courage. You never tried to walk the journey for me. You simply made sure I never had to walk it alone.

More than anything else, you loved me through it all. You gave me courage when I was afraid, hope when I felt discouraged, strength when I felt weak, and laughter when I needed it most.

Thank you for being my caregiver, my greatest supporter, my best friend, and the love of my life.

I could not have walked this journey without you.

With all my love,

Joann

What Others Are Saying

Weighing in On Hypnosis

Weighing in on Hypnosis is a 'must read' if you are seeking a permanent weight loss solution that taps into your wonderful mind power. Joann Abrahamsen teaches you how to use self-hypnosis to rewire your mindset, make habit change easy and seemingly magical, and you also learn a new life skill in the process. Inside these pages you'll discover the learnings and observations Joann shares from her own weight loss journey, in a way that is easy to follow and apply to your own weight loss success. Her promise is real: in my own words, a new you will, indeed, emerge as you take back control and feel better each day as you make steady progress toward your ideal weight. I especially like that she emphasizes the importance of a good night's sleep. Her advice is on target.

Robert Martel, Professional Hypnotist, and Author of I Am Sleeping Now, and The Magic of Aesop

What makes *Weighing in on Hypnosis* stand out is Joann Abrahamsen's ability to blend professional insight with heartfelt storytelling. As a fellow hypnotist, I see the value in every chapter. It's a gift to both practitioners and anyone ready to change their relationship with food and self.

Dan Candell, The Anxiety Relief Guy, Hypnotist, Motivational Speaker, Author of 5 Minute Stress Relief for Professionals.

Self-Hypnosis: Easy as 1, 2, 3: 3 Minutes to Change Your Life

"This book is unique, and the self-hypnosis method Joann offers is amazing! You will formulate your own powerful suggestions based on the habit(s) you want to change and apply them in just three minutes. It's like speed-trance for self-hypnosis! Her book includes suggestions for weight management, stopping smoking, peak performance, sales, memory and learning, and many other applications. Joann's book delivers on the promise that in just three minutes a day, you can change just about anything."

Dr. Richard Nongard, author of *The Self-Hypnosis* Solution and *Excellence in Ericksonian Hypnotherapy*

"Joann Abrahamsen has created one of the easiest self-hypnosis books I have ever read. Her sub-title says it all: 3 Minutes to Change Your Life! Without spending too much time, you learn the self-hypnosis skills quickly and apply them easily. Joann relates to her readers with her easy style and clear writing. She discusses and demystifies hypnosis and talks a little bit about how she became involved with hypnosis. I plan on recommending this book to my students and clients. Read this book to learn how easy it can be to change your life and become the person you want to be in three easy steps."

Larry Garrett, certified consulting hypnotist and author of Healing the Enemy and Hypnotizing the Devil

Other books by Joann Abrahamsen

Self-Hypnosis: Easy as 1, 2, 3; 3 Minutes to Change Your Life

A Potpourri of Hypnotic Techniques: Adding the WOW Factor to your Practice

Weighing in on Hypnosis: Lifestyle and Habit Changes for Weight Loss Success

Contact the Author

Thank you for reading *The Rainbow After the Storm: Surviving and Thriving After a Cancer Diagnosis.*

I sincerely hope this book has brought you comfort, encouragement, and practical tools to help you or someone you love navigate the cancer journey.

I always enjoy hearing from readers. Whether you would like to share your story, ask a question, comment on the book, or inquire about presentations, workshops, or hypnosis training, I would be delighted to hear from you.

I would love to hear your story. If this book has touched your life or helped you in some way, please consider writing to me. Your message may encourage me just as much as I hope this book has encouraged you.

You can reach me at:

Email: joann4@optonline.net Please put "cancer book" in the subject line

Website: www.joannabrahamsen.com

Facebook: Facebook/Joann Polizzi Abrahamsen Fried

Instagram: https://www.instagram.com/joannabrahamsen

Thank you again for allowing me to be part of your journey.

With warmest wishes for health, hope, and happiness,

Joann Abrahamsen

"May you always find your rainbow after the storm."

TABLE OF CONTENTS

Foreword

By Larry Garrett

I searched for the right phrase to draw you into this book, and one came immediately to mind: "The wounded duckling makes the best healer." Joann Abrahamsen is that healer. Who better to teach us how to heal than someone who has walked through the fire of this dreaded disease herself?

There was an Oldsmobile commercial in the 1960s that always stayed with me because of its simple but powerful message. It showed a person standing beside their car, hand resting on the front fender, saying: "Ask the person who drives one." Joann has driven this road. She understands cancer and healing not from theory, but from lived experience. She has faced the deepest fears that come with hearing the words "you have cancer," and now she shares with you, the reader, ways to cope, heal, and continue living life fully.

For many people, cancer feels like a monster hiding in the shadows—something feared even when it has not touched their lives directly. If you have had cancer, love someone who has cancer, or live with the fear of cancer, Joann's words will help you move forward. She teaches that the greatest fear is often fear itself.

Personally, I have had my own experience with cancer, and I am honored to share a few words to encourage you to read every page of Joann Abrahamsen's book, *The Rainbow After the Storm.* Before I ever faced cancer myself, I used to give presentations to a breast cancer survivors' group in Chicago called *Why Me?* Eventually, thankfully, they changed the name. I remember preparing to speak to that group about staying positive, and I felt incredibly nervous. What did I know? I had never had cancer. How could I speak about something I had never experienced? As I was getting ready to leave, my phone rang—this was back in the landline days, before cell phones. It was my mother. I told her I was running late because I was preparing to speak to a cancer survivors' group and wasn't sure how to approach it. She immediately became excited and said, "Tell them my story."

My mother had been diagnosed with breast cancer in 1969, when cancer treatment was far more primitive than it is today. Her oncologist told her to prepare for the inevitable because she likely would not live long. She underwent a radical mastectomy, which at that time commonly involved removing the entire breast, chest wall muscles, and lymph nodes. She later told me that after hearing her prognosis, she lay in bed feeling as though her life was slipping away. Then she had a powerful realization. She said to herself: "I can't die. I have two sons and a husband who need me." My mother lived another forty years. During those years, she faced cancer four more times—and survived.

What is it that we fear so deeply about this word: **cancer**? I found myself confronting that question in March of 2020. Many people remember March 2020 as the beginning of COVID. I barely noticed COVID. I had just been told I had throat cancer. While the world was focused on the pandemic, I was trying to find doctors while medical offices were shutting down. As a hypnotist who depends on his voice, hearing the words *throat cancer* was especially frightening. But one phrase carried me through the greatest healing journey of my life: "Don't fight the cancer—you will lose. Learn to know the cancer so you can heal." That mindset changed everything for me. And in what seemed like an unbelievable coincidence—or perhaps something greater—my middle son, Scott, who was fifty-three at the time, was diagnosed with melanoma during the very same week. Melanoma is one of the most serious forms of skin cancer, yet it is highly treatable when caught early. My son and I went through treatment at the same time. And we healed at nearly the same time. What carried us through was the positive dialogue we created together. We learned to understand the cancer rather than live in constant fear of it.

Joann, through her heartfelt writing, will guide you through every step of your own healing journey. Her words offer hope. They offer strength. They offer practical tools for healing. And most importantly, they remind you that life is still waiting for you after the storm.

Enjoy her words.

Find your strength.

And heal.

This book will help you do exactly that.

Why Read This Book?

If you're holding this book, chances are cancer has touched your life in some way. Perhaps you've just been diagnosed. Maybe you're in the middle of treatment, recovering from treatment, living with metastatic cancer, or caring for someone you love. Wherever you are on this journey, I want you to know one thing:

You are not alone.

I wrote this book because I've been where you are. I know what it feels like to hear the words, "You have cancer." I know the fear, the uncertainty, the endless waiting, and the questions that keep you awake at night. But I also know something else.

I know that it is possible to find hope in the middle of fear, strength when you feel weak, laughter on difficult days, and joy even while living with cancer.

This is not a medical textbook. It's a companion for the journey.

Within these pages, I'll share my own experiences with breast cancer—the challenges I faced, the lessons I learned, and the strategies that helped me not only survive but truly thrive. I'll also introduce you to other cancer survivors whose stories remind us that every journey is unique, yet none of us has to walk it alone.

As a hypnotist for more than thirty years, I'll also share simple mind-body techniques, including hypnosis, that can help reduce stress, ease anxiety, improve sleep, manage discomfort, and help you regain a sense of calm and control during an often overwhelming time.

You don't have to read this book from cover to cover. Start with the chapters that speak to your needs today. Return to others when you're ready. Let this book be a source of encouragement whenever you need it.

Most of all, I hope you'll come away with this message:

A cancer diagnosis may change your life, but it doesn't have to take away your hope, your purpose, or your ability to live fully.

There will be storms along the way. Some will be gentle showers, while others may feel overwhelming. But storms do pass. And when they do, if you look carefully, you may discover something beautiful waiting on the other side.

If this book helps you feel a little less afraid, a little more hopeful, and a little more confident that brighter days are ahead, then sharing my journey will have been worth it.

My hope is that this book will help you find your own rainbow after the storm.

Introduction

You may have picked up this book because you have been diagnosed with cancer, are in treatment, are a cancer survivor, or are a caregiver. Whatever your reason, you need this book.

I was diagnosed with Stage I breast cancer in May of 2020. Getting the "Big C" diagnosis is one of the most life-altering experiences you could ever have, but it does not need to be the most defining. It's natural to feel a rush of fear, anxiety, or sadness in those first moments—but what you do after that is when your healing begins.

Take a deep breath, try to relax, and remind yourself there is much that can be done. The sooner you realize that cancer is a word, not a sentence, the sooner you can begin your healing journey. Take time to gather information, research your options, and make thoughtful decisions about your care.

I am not a doctor or a medical professional, and I don't claim to be an expert. My purpose in writing this book is simple: by sharing my story, along with the stories of my clients and my family, I hope to encourage you to embrace your diagnosis with courage, lean on the tools that support you, and push through—no matter what.

Although my personal focus is on breast cancer, the lessons and techniques here are not limited to one diagnosis. Cancer touches so many lives in different ways, and this book can be helpful to anyone—no matter what type of cancer you or your loved ones are facing.

Cancer runs in my family. My father had prostate cancer that spread to his bladder, my mother was diagnosed with colon cancer in her 90s, and my maternal aunt faced breast cancer in her early 50s. Their journeys were very different, and yet each carried lessons of strength, courage, and acceptance. You'll find their stories here, too, as reminders that no two journeys are the same, but every journey can hold meaning and inspiration.

One of the most important tools I relied on during my treatment was hypnosis. Hypnosis is not mind control or a stage trick—it is a natural state of focused attention and deep relaxation. In this state, the mind becomes more receptive to helpful suggestions, allowing you to calm fear, reduce discomfort, and even change the way you experience time and pain. I used self-hypnosis throughout my cancer journey—in the biopsy room, during chemotherapy, and while lying perfectly still for radiation, MRIs, CAT scans, etc.

Humor often walked hand-in-hand with hypnosis, helping me lighten the moment and connect with the people caring for me. One of my favorite memories was during an initial needle biopsy. I was being wheeled into the procedure room in a hospital gown, chatting with the attending doctor. I explained that I was a hypnotist and would be using hypnosis to reduce the discomfort.

She was fascinated and asked me for a business card. I pretended to feel for pockets in my gown, and we both burst out laughing. That laughter eased the tension for both of us, making the whole experience a little lighter.

Later, during chemotherapy, I leaned on hypnosis again. I have rolling veins, which can make needle insertion tricky. I would tell the nurse, "I have rolling veins, but that shouldn't be a problem for an expert such as yourself. And don't worry—I'll be using self-hypnosis to numb the area." If they weren't confident, they called in someone more experienced; if they were, they often grew fascinated and asked me questions afterward.

Although my personal journey began with a diagnosis of breast cancer, the lessons in this book extend far beyond one disease. While writing these pages, I have had the privilege of hearing the stories of individuals facing different types of cancer. Their experiences, woven together with my own, remind us that although every cancer journey is unique, the emotions, fears, hopes, and triumphs are remarkably similar. Throughout this book, you will meet people who faced uncertainty with courage, found moments of laughter in the midst of difficult days, and discovered hope when they least expected it. Along the way, I will share how hypnosis became an invaluable tool in my own cancer journey and in helping Joanne face hers. In many of the other stories, I will also suggest ways hypnosis could have been used to ease fear, reduce anxiety, manage discomfort, and enhance emotional well-being during treatment. Whether you are living with breast cancer, prostate cancer, throat cancer, colon cancer, or another diagnosis, I hope these stories—and the practical strategies and insights they offer—will remind you that you are never alone. My wish is that this book will inspire you to navigate your own journey with greater confidence, resilience, and hope—one step, one laugh, and one breath at a time.

Chapter 1

One Ordinary Shower

The Day Everything Changed

Cancer doesn't always announce itself with dramatic symptoms. Sometimes it begins in the most ordinary way.

At the beginning of every month, I made it a habit to perform a breast self-examination. It was simply part of my self-care routine—something I had done for years without giving it much thought.

One ordinary day in February, while taking an ordinary shower, I examined my breasts as I always did. That's when I felt it.

A tiny lump—about the size of a pea—just to the left of my nipple in my left breast.

I remember thinking, *"I don't think that was there last month."*

I was already scheduled for my annual mammogram at the end of the month, but something told me not to wait. I called and was able to move the appointment up to the middle of February.

To my surprise, the mammogram didn't show the little "pea" I had felt. Fortunately, the radiologist decided to do a sonogram as well. That ultrasound clearly revealed the suspicious area.

The radiologist told me, "It's a good thing you came in when you did. This likely wouldn't have shown up on the mammogram yet, and by the time of your next screening, it could have had months to grow."

Those words have stayed with me ever since.

Next came the biopsy, genetic counseling, and testing for the BRCA gene mutation. The results showed that I did not carry the BRCA mutation. However, because of my strong family history of cancer, my oncologist recommended an aggressive treatment plan. She wanted to give me the best possible chance for a cure, so my treatment included surgery, chemotherapy, and radiation.

Looking back, I often think about that ordinary shower.

Had I skipped my monthly self-examination or decided to wait until my scheduled mammogram, my story might have been very different.

That tiny pea-sized lump changed the course of my life. It taught me one of the greatest lessons of my cancer journey: never underestimate the importance of knowing your own body. No one knows what is normal for you better than you do. Routine screenings and mammograms are essential, but so is paying attention when something doesn't feel quite right. Sometimes, listening to that quiet inner voice and taking action promptly can make all the difference. One ordinary shower became the reason I am here to tell my story today, and I hope it inspires you to take charge of your own health as well.

Chapter 2

Discovery

Receiving the Diagnosis

You have cancer!

My husband, Robert, said I turned ash grey, my blood pressure dropped, and the oncologist and the physician's assistant wanted me to go to the emergency room.

My diagnosis came in May 2020 at the beginning of the COVID-19 pandemic. There was NO WAY I was going to the emergency room. I did not want to catch Covid on top of the cancer. They gave me crackers and water, but still my blood pressure did not normalize. Robert convinced me to go to the ER. I did and I was OK after a half an hour.

Getting the "Big C" diagnosis is one of the most life-altering experiences you could ever have, but it does not need to be the most defining.

This was not my first cancer diagnosis. Not my first cancer. In 2008 I was diagnosed with kidney cancer. I had surgery to remove part of my right kidney, but I did not need chemo or radiation. But breast cancer was different.

It's a natural part of the journey to feel the rush of difficult emotions following the moment you learn about the diagnosis, but what you do after that moment is when your healing begins.

Take a deep breath, try to relax, and remind yourself there is lots that can be done.

Try to view this moment as a pivotal point of your life, where you allow your strengths to come alive to face your fears. The sooner you realize that the big "C" is a word, and not a sentence, the sooner you can begin your healing journey.

Take time to gather as much information as you can and research all your options before deciding on the course of action that is best for you.

As you attempt to get the best results, we feel it is important that you start in the right way and that starts with getting the right testing.

Many people remember the exact moment they heard the words. Even if everything else around that time feels blurry, they remember that moment.

It may have been something the doctor said. A phone call that lasted only minutes. Sitting in a parking lot afterward, staring ahead, trying to understand how life could feel so different in the span of a single conversation.

Life does not always change dramatically or loudly. Sometimes it changes quietly, with one sentence spoken calmly while everything else in the room remains exactly the same.

For some people, the moment feels overwhelming. The heart races. Thoughts scatter in every direction. The body reacts before the mind can even begin to process what has happened. For others, the experience feels strangely quiet. Almost numb. As though the words floated past them without fully landing. Both responses are normal.

For me, it was shock. When we are confronted with life-changing news, the mind and body instinctively try to protect us. Shock is not weakness. It is a very human response to overwhelming information.

I kept thinking, "What did I do or didn't do to get cancer?" Whose "fault" was this?

In the hours and days after a diagnosis, many people describe feeling disconnected from reality. You may go through your normal routines while feeling oddly distant from them. You may replay conversations repeatedly, trying to remember exact words, tone, or expressions. You may wonder if you heard things correctly. You may also notice that time feels different. Waiting feels heavier. Ordinary tasks take more effort. You may feel exhausted even though you have done very little.

This is not laziness. It is not avoidance. It is your nervous system trying to absorb something enormous. Some people feel an urgent need to act immediately. They begin researching, making phone calls, organizing plans, searching for answers. Action can temporarily create a sense of control. Others feel frozen, unable to make even simple decisions because they do not know where to begin. I began researching.

The first days after diagnosis are not meant to be productive. They are meant to help you absorb reality at a pace your mind and body can tolerate.

Many people become very hard on themselves during this stage. You may think you should be asking better questions. You may feel guilty for not reacting the "right" way. You may wonder why you cannot stop crying — or why you are not crying at all.

There is no correct emotional response to a cancer diagnosis.

Fear does not mean you are weak. Calmness does not mean you do not care. Numbness does not mean denial.

Each response reflects the way your system is coping in that moment.

One of the hardest parts of this stage is uncertainty. You may have received incomplete information. Or far too much information all at once. You may know the diagnosis but not yet understand the details or what comes next.

Uncertainty is often more frightening than facts.

The mind naturally tries to fill in the blanks, and unfortunately it often fills them with worst-case scenarios. Thoughts jump far ahead into imagined futures that may never happen.

This is why nighttime can feel especially difficult. During the day there are distractions. At night, thoughts grow louder.

If this is happening to you, it does not mean you are failing to cope. It means you are human.

Another difficult adjustment is the sudden shift in identity. You may not think of yourself as a "patient." The word may feel foreign, uncomfortable, or unreal. You may still feel like yourself while simultaneously feeling changed in ways you cannot yet explain.

There is no rush to define yourself.

You are allowed to take your time understanding what this diagnosis means to you personally. You are allowed to feel normal one moment and completely overwhelmed the next.

Both experiences can exist together.

During these early days, people around you may react in surprising ways. Some may become overly anxious or controlling. Others may minimize the situation because they do not know how to tolerate their own fear. Some people may disappear altogether because they do not know what to say.

Their reactions are often about their own discomfort, not their lack of caring. Even so, it can still feel painful.

You may suddenly feel responsible for managing everyone else's emotions while still trying to manage your own.

Please hear this clearly:

You are not responsible for carrying everyone emotionally right now.

Your primary responsibility in these early days is your own well-being.

You do not owe anyone constant updates, explanations, reassurance, or emotional energy unless you choose to give it. It is okay to protect your peace. It is okay to step back from conversations that drain you.

You may also notice physical changes from stress and shock. Sleep may become difficult. Appetite may disappear or increase. Your body may feel tense, restless, heavy, or exhausted.

These are common stress responses.

Your nervous system has received information that it interprets as threat, and it is trying to adjust.

This is a time for gentleness.

If possible, focus on very basic care. Drink water. Eat something simple. Rest when you can. Sit outside for a few minutes. Take a short walk. Breathe slowly.

These small acts may seem insignificant, but they help calm and regulate the nervous system.

One of the most important things to understand during this phase is what you do not need to do.

You do not need to understand your entire treatment plan immediately.

You do not need to make every decision today.

You do not need to read every article, statistic, or online forum.

Too much information too quickly can increase fear instead of creating clarity.

Many people later say they regret falling deeply into internet searches during those first frightened days. While the internet contains valuable information, it also contains outdated statistics, extreme cases, and stories that may have absolutely nothing to do with your situation.

Without guidance, it becomes easy to confuse possibility with probability.

This book will help you approach information in a safer, calmer, and more balanced way.

For now, it is enough to simply acknowledge what has happened.

You have received news that changes the way you see the future. That takes time to process.

You may feel pressure to "be strong."

But strength does not mean suppressing fear.

Strength does not mean pretending everything is fine.

Strength does not mean having immediate answers.

Sometimes strength simply means allowing yourself to feel what you feel without judging yourself for it.

Sometimes strength means taking one breath, one hour, one step at a time.

Some people worry that acknowledging fear will make it worse. In reality, fear often becomes louder when it is ignored.

You may find it helpful to quietly say to yourself:

"This is hard."
"This is frightening."
"I am allowed to feel this way."

There is no prize for rushing emotional acceptance.

Acceptance unfolds gradually and unevenly. Some days you may feel calm and grounded. Other days you may feel angry, frightened, or resistant.

That does not mean you are failing. It means you are processing.

At this stage, many people wonder if life will ever feel normal again.

Life may not return to the exact version of normal you once knew. But that does not mean life stops.

Over time, many people slowly discover a new rhythm. Not immediately. Not perfectly. But gradually.

You do not need to imagine that future right now.

Right now, your task is much simpler.

Acknowledge what has happened.

Care for yourself gently.

Do not force emotional clarity before it naturally arrives.

This chapter is not meant to push you forward before you are ready.

It is meant to help you stand still for a moment without feeling like you are falling apart.

In the next chapter, we will talk about information — what matters now, what can wait, and how to avoid becoming emotionally overloaded during this early stage.

For now, just pause.

Chapter 3

Understanding My Diagnosis

Taking it one step at a time

After my biopsy confirmed that I had breast cancer, I suddenly found myself learning an entirely new language. My pathology report was filled with words and abbreviations I had never heard before. I didn't really care what all the letters stood for. What I wanted to know was much simpler: *What does this mean, and how are we going to treat it?*

My oncologist explained that I had **Stage IB invasive lobular carcinoma**, the second most common type of breast cancer. At first, it appeared that I had one tumor in my left breast. During surgery, however, my surgeon discovered there were actually four separate tumors. Two nearby lymph nodes were also removed, and both contained cancer cells. Although that news was frightening, I was relieved to learn that there was no evidence the cancer had spread to other parts of my body.

There was encouraging news as well. My cancer was **hormone receptor-positive** and **HER2-negative**, meaning there were highly effective treatments available to reduce the chance of it returning. A specialized test called the Oncotype DX also suggested that my risk of recurrence was relatively low.

After reviewing all of my test results, my oncology team recommended a treatment plan that included surgery, four rounds of chemotherapy, radiation therapy, and hormone-blocking medication.

At first, all I heard was a long list of treatments. It felt overwhelming. But I soon learned that each recommendation had a specific purpose. Surgery removed the cancer that could be seen. Chemotherapy was designed to destroy any microscopic cancer cells that might have escaped into my bloodstream or lymphatic system. Radiation would treat the breast itself, helping destroy any remaining cancer cells in that area. Finally, hormone therapy would continue working for years by reducing the estrogen that fueled my particular type of breast cancer.

Looking back, understanding *why* each treatment was recommended helped me feel less afraid. Instead of seeing four separate hurdles, I began to see one carefully planned strategy designed to give me the very best chance of living a long, healthy life.

Chapter 4

After the Diagnosis

Questions to ask

After a breast cancer diagnosis, many people leave the first oncology appointment realizing they forgot to ask half the questions they wanted answered. Bringing a written list to your first appointment after the diagnosis can help you feel more organized and informed during a time that often feels overwhelming. I created a notebook and brought this to all my appointments. Bringing someone with you also helps. I had my husband Robert come with me to my appointments. You will have a team of doctors and physician assistants working with you. My team includes a breast cancer surgeon, an oncologist, and a radiologist. Here are important questions to consider asking your oncologist:

Understanding the Diagnosis

- What type of breast cancer do I have?
- What stage is the cancer?

- Has the cancer spread beyond the breast or lymph nodes?
- What does my pathology report mean?
- What is the tumor grade?
- Is the cancer hormone receptor-positive or HER2-positive?
- How aggressive does this cancer appear to be?

Treatment Planning

- What treatment options do you recommend for me?
- What is the goal of treatment — cure, control, or prevention of recurrence?
- Will I need surgery, chemotherapy, radiation, hormone therapy, immunotherapy, or targeted therapy?
- In what order will treatments happen?
- How soon do I need to begin treatment?
- Should I get a second opinion?

Surgery Questions

- Do I need a lumpectomy or mastectomy?
- Will lymph nodes be removed?
- Am I a candidate for breast reconstruction?
- What are the risks and recovery times for surgery?
- How might surgery affect my appearance or arm mobility?

Chemotherapy & Medication Questions

- Why are you recommending chemotherapy (or not)?
- What side effects are most common?
- Will I lose my hair?
- Could treatment affect my heart, nerves, or memory?
- Will treatment put me into menopause?
- Are there medications to help with side effects?

Radiation Questions

- Will I need radiation therapy?
- How many treatments are typical?
- What side effects should I expect?
- Could radiation affect my skin, lungs, or heart?

Prognosis & Outcomes

- What is my prognosis?
- What are the chances of recurrence?
- How will we monitor for recurrence after treatment?
- Are there lifestyle changes that may improve outcomes?

Daily Life & Practical Concerns

- Will I be able to work during treatment?
- Can I exercise?
- Are there foods or supplements I should avoid?
- How will treatment affect intimacy or fertility?
- Should I speak with a genetic counselor?
- Are there clinical trials appropriate for me?

Support & Resources

- Is there an oncology nurse navigator or social worker available?
- Are support groups available?
- Where can I find reliable information?
- What symptoms should prompt an urgent call to your office?

You may also want to ask:

- "If this were your family member, what would you recommend?"

- "What are the most important decisions I need to make right now?"

Many patients find it helpful to:

- Bring a trusted person to appointments
- Record the conversation (with permission)
- Keep a notebook or binder with reports, medications, and questions
- Ask for copies of pathology and imaging reports

Asking questions does not mean you are being difficult—it means you are becoming an informed partner in your own care. No one expects you to remember everything or understand every medical term after hearing the words, "You have cancer." Take your time. Write down your questions. Bring someone you trust with you. Ask your doctors to explain things in language you can understand, and don't hesitate to ask them to repeat something if it isn't clear.

Remember, this is your body, your treatment, and your journey. The more informed you are, the more confident you will feel when making important decisions. One step at a time, one question at a time, you will find your way forward.

In the next chapter, I'll introduce you to the members of the cancer care team who walked beside me throughout my treatment and explain the important role each one played in my recovery.

Chapter 5

Your Cancer Care Team

You Don't Have to Remember Who Everyone Is

One of the things that surprised me after my breast cancer diagnosis was how quickly my medical world grew. Almost overnight, I found myself meeting doctor after doctor, nurse after nurse, and specialist after specialist. At times, it felt as though everyone was speaking a language I didn't yet understand.

The good news is that you don't have to remember who everyone is or what each person does all at once. Your healthcare team is there to guide you through each step of your treatment. Every member has a specific role, and together they work to provide the best care possible.

My own team included a breast surgeon, a medical oncologist, a radiation oncologist, a radiologist, a pathologist, a physical therapist, and many wonderful nurses and other healthcare professionals who cared for me throughout my treatment.

Looking back, I realized I wasn't facing cancer alone. I had an entire team walking beside me.

Not every person diagnosed with cancer will see all of the specialists listed below, but understanding their roles can help make the process feel a little less overwhelming.

Primary Care Physician

Your primary care physician is your regular doctor. Even while your cancer specialists are directing your treatment, your primary care physician continues to oversee your general health, manage other medical conditions, and coordinate care when needed.

Breast Surgeon (Surgical Oncologist)

For many people, this is one of the first specialists they meet after receiving a diagnosis. A breast surgeon performs procedures such as biopsies, lumpectomies, or mastectomies and helps determine the most appropriate surgical treatment.

Medical Oncologist

The medical oncologist is often the physician who oversees your overall cancer treatment plan. This doctor determines whether chemotherapy, hormone therapy, targeted therapy, immunotherapy, or other medications are recommended and monitors your progress throughout treatment.

Radiation Oncologist

If radiation therapy is part of your treatment plan, the radiation oncologist designs and supervises those treatments. Their goal is to destroy any remaining cancer cells while protecting as much healthy tissue as possible.

Plastic and Reconstructive Surgeon

Some people choose breast reconstruction following surgery. If reconstruction is an option you are considering, a plastic surgeon can explain the different procedures available and help you decide what is best for you.

Radiologist

Radiologists interpret imaging studies such as mammograms, breast ultrasounds, MRIs, CT scans, PET scans, and other imaging tests that help diagnose, stage, and monitor cancer.

Pathologist

Although you may never meet your pathologist, this physician plays a vital role in your care. The pathologist carefully examines tissue removed during your biopsy or surgery and prepares the pathology report that identifies the type of cancer, tumor grade, hormone receptor status (ER and PR), HER2 status, and other important information that helps guide treatment decisions.

Genetic Counselor

Some patients are referred to a genetic counselor to determine whether inherited gene mutations, such as BRCA1 or BRCA2, may have contributed to their cancer. The results can sometimes influence treatment decisions and may provide important information for family members.

Fertility Specialist

Younger adults who hope to have children in the future may wish to meet with a fertility specialist before beginning chemotherapy or hormone therapy, as some treatments can affect fertility.

Oncology Nurses and Nurse Navigators

Although they are not physicians, oncology nurses and nurse navigators often become some of the most important members of your healthcare team. They answer questions, explain treatments, coordinate appointments, provide education, and offer reassurance during what can be an overwhelming time.

Lymphedema Specialists and Physical Therapists

Following surgery or lymph node removal, some patients work with therapists specially trained to prevent or treat lymphedema, improve range of motion, and help restore strength and function. I was fortunate to work with an outstanding lymphedema therapist whose guidance made a tremendous difference in my recovery.

Integrative Medicine Specialists

Many cancer centers also offer supportive services such as nutrition counseling, acupuncture, massage therapy, meditation, stress management, or other complementary approaches designed to help patients cope with treatment and improve their quality of life.

Mental Health Professionals

A cancer diagnosis affects much more than the body. Psychologists, counselors, social workers, and psychiatrists can help patients and their families manage fear, anxiety, depression, and the many emotions that often accompany a cancer diagnosis.

Palliative Care Specialists

Many people mistakenly believe palliative care is only for the end of life. In reality, these specialists focus on improving quality of life at any stage of cancer by helping patients manage pain, fatigue, nausea, anxiety, and other symptoms so they can feel as well as possible during treatment.

Many cancer centers use what is called a **multidisciplinary team** approach. Rather than working independently, your doctors regularly communicate with one another, review your test results, and discuss the treatment plan that is best suited to your individual situation. Knowing that experienced professionals were working together on my behalf gave me confidence that I was receiving the best care possible.

As you begin meeting with your healthcare team, you'll probably hear unfamiliar words and medical terms. You may hear phrases such as:

- Tumor board
- ER-positive or PR-positive
- HER2-positive
- Triple-negative breast cancer
- Stage
- Grade

At first, it may feel like everyone is speaking a foreign language. That's completely normal.

You are not expected to understand everything during your first few appointments. In fact, most people don't. Don't hesitate to ask questions, ask your doctor to repeat something, or ask for an explanation in simpler language. I found it helpful to keep a notebook with me at every appointment so I could write down important information and questions. I also brought my husband, Robert, with me whenever possible. There were times when one of us heard something the other had missed. Having another set of ears—and another source of support—made a tremendous difference.

Remember, your healthcare team isn't just treating your cancer. They're there to support you throughout your journey. Never be afraid to ask questions. The more you understand, the more confident and empowered you'll feel as you move forward.

Chapter 6

Surgery—The First Step Toward Healing

Preparing for Surgery, Recovery, and What to Expect

After hearing the words, *"You have cancer,"* life seemed to shift into fast forward. Suddenly there were appointments with my breast surgeon, my medical oncologist, imaging studies, blood work, and more information than I ever imagined I could absorb. I found myself learning an entirely new language—biopsies, pathology reports, hormone receptors, sentinel lymph nodes, and treatment plans. As overwhelming as it all felt, one thing became clear.

Surgery would be the first major step in treating my breast cancer.

For many people diagnosed with breast cancer, surgery is the cornerstone of treatment. While chemotherapy, radiation, hormone therapy, or targeted therapy may also be recommended, surgery is often the first active step in removing the cancer from the body.

Like many newly diagnosed patients, I had countless questions. What exactly would the surgeon remove? Would the cancer be gone? How long would recovery take? Would I wake up feeling different? Would there be pain? Even though my surgeon carefully explained everything, I still found myself wondering what surgery would actually be like.

If you're preparing for surgery yourself, please know these feelings are completely normal. Nearly everyone experiences some degree of fear and uncertainty before an operation. The unknown can be frightening. Fortunately, once I understood what to expect, much of that fear began to fade.

Understanding the Different Types of Surgery

Not everyone with breast cancer has the same operation. The type of surgery depends on several factors, including the size and location of the tumor, whether there are multiple tumors, the stage of the cancer, your overall health, your personal preferences, and your surgeon's recommendations.

Some women have a lumpectomy, sometimes called breast-conserving surgery, in which only the tumor and a small amount of surrounding healthy tissue are removed. Others choose—or require—a mastectomy, in which the entire breast is removed. Some women also decide to have breast reconstruction either immediately following surgery or at a later time.

In addition to removing the breast tumor, many patients also have one or more lymph nodes removed from under the arm. These lymph nodes help determine whether cancer cells have spread beyond the breast and provide valuable information that guides future treatment decisions.

Every person's surgery is unique, but the goal is always the same—to remove the cancer while giving you the best possible chance for a healthy future.

My Surgery

On July 14, 2020, I underwent surgery to remove my breast cancer.

Before surgery, my cancer had been classified as Stage I. Like most patients, I hoped the operation would remove the cancer and that would be the end of my story.

Unfortunately, the final pathology report revealed something different.

Instead of finding one tumor, my surgeon discovered four separate tumors within my breast. In addition, two sentinel lymph nodes tested positive for cancer. Because the cancer had spread to those lymph nodes, my diagnosis was changed from Stage I to Stage IB breast cancer.

Hearing that news was difficult.

Like so many patients, I had hoped surgery would bring certainty and relief. Instead, it answered some questions while raising new ones.

Looking back now, however, I see it very differently.

The surgery didn't simply remove my cancer. It gave my medical team the information they needed to design the treatment plan that ultimately gave me the best chance for a healthy future. Although the pathology report wasn't what I had hoped for, it provided exactly the information my doctors needed to recommend the next steps in my treatment.

Sometimes the answers we receive aren't the answers we want.

But they are the answers we need.

Waiting for the Final Pathology Report

One thing many people don't realize is that surgery doesn't answer every question immediately.

After surgery comes another period of waiting while the pathology report is completed. During that time, specialists carefully examine the tissue and lymph nodes under a microscope. Their findings determine the exact stage of the cancer and help your medical team decide whether additional treatments—such as chemotherapy, radiation, hormone therapy, or targeted therapy—are needed.

Waiting can be one of the hardest parts of the entire cancer journey.

Your mind naturally begins filling in the blanks with endless *"what ifs."*

I certainly experienced those moments myself.

But I also realized something important.

No amount of worrying could change the pathology report.

It could only rob me of today's peace.

This became another opportunity to practice the very skills I had taught my hypnosis clients for years—staying grounded in the present moment rather than imagining frightening possibilities that might never happen.

Whenever I found my thoughts racing ahead, I gently reminded myself to come back to today.

One breath.

One moment.

One day at a time.

That simple shift helped me remain calmer while I waited for answers that would come soon enough.

Preparing for Surgery

Although surgery can feel frightening, there are several things that helped me feel more prepared.

I packed a small bag with everything I thought I might need and chose comfortable clothing that would be easy to put on afterward. Button-front shirts and zip-up sweatshirts are much easier than trying to pull clothing over your head during those first few days after breast surgery.

I also made sure my home was ready before I left for the hospital. Prescriptions were filled, frequently used items were placed within easy reach, and I tried to think ahead about anything that might make my recovery easier.

Although I didn't have to worry about taking time off from work because I had retired in 2018, I often thought about those who were trying to juggle cancer treatments while continuing to meet their work obligations. My heart truly went out to them. Facing cancer is difficult enough without the added stress of balancing doctor appointments, treatments, recovery, and the responsibilities of a job.

One of the best things I did before surgery was prepare for life after I came home.

That included making sure meals would be one less thing to worry about.

I'll let you in on a little secret—Robert loves to cook, so I happily let him.

When we were first married, Robert announced that he wanted to be the primary cook in our household.

I smiled and replied, "You know, I like to cook too. I'd like to make dinner once in a while."

Without missing a beat, he said, "Anytime you want to cook, just let me know, and the kitchen is yours."

Well...

A year and a half later, I finally took him up on his offer and made baked ziti and meatballs.

To this day, we still laugh about it.

Needless to say, Robert remained the chief cook in our home, and I had absolutely no complaints. Knowing that wonderful meals would be waiting for me after surgery gave me one less thing to worry about and one more reason to focus completely on healing.

Perhaps the hardest part of preparing for surgery wasn't packing my bag or organizing the house.

It was learning to accept help.

Like many people, I had spent most of my life taking care of others. Allowing family and friends to care for me didn't come naturally.

Yet looking back, accepting their kindness became one of the greatest lessons of my cancer journey.

Sometimes allowing others to help isn't a sign of weakness.

It's a gift you give to them...

and to yourself.

The Day of Surgery

My surgery was scheduled for **7:00 a.m.,** which meant I had to be at the hospital by **6:00 a.m.**

Groan!

If you know me, you know I have never been a morning person. Even when I was working, I arranged a flexible schedule so I could work from **10:00 a.m. to 6:00 p.m.** Getting up early has never been one of my favorite things.

I think my dislike of early mornings goes all the way back to childhood. Saturdays were my favorite because I could finally sleep in. My brother would try everything he could think of to coax me out of bed to watch Saturday morning cartoons, but I usually preferred staying under the covers just a little longer.

Ironically, after all those years of avoiding early mornings, there I was willingly arriving at the hospital before sunrise.

Somehow, on that day, getting up early didn't seem nearly as important as getting well.

Robert drove me to the hospital that morning and stayed with me in the pre-operative area, holding my hand until it was time for me to go into the operating room. His calm presence was incredibly reassuring, and knowing he was there made it a little easier to face the unknown.

As the nurses prepared me for surgery, I was once again reminded how fortunate I was to be surrounded by kind, compassionate healthcare professionals. They answered my questions, explained what would happen next, and treated me with genuine warmth and respect. Those simple acts of kindness helped calm my fears more than they probably realized.

Although I had spent more than thirty years teaching hypnosis to others, I found myself relying on those same techniques. I focused on my breathing, pictured myself feeling calm and safe, and reminded myself that I was in capable hands. Rather than imagining everything that could go wrong, I chose to picture a successful surgery and a smooth recovery.

There comes a moment before every surgery when you realize there is nothing more you need to do.

You have asked your questions.

You have made your decisions.

You have placed your trust in your surgeon and your medical team.

All that's left is to let go and allow them to do what they have spent years training to do.

That was the moment I experienced as I was wheeled toward the operating room.

I took one slow, deep breath and silently reminded myself:

"Everything is going to be all right."

I don't remember anything about the surgery itself.

The next thing I remember was opening my eyes in the recovery room and seeing the first face that greeted me—Robert's smiling face.

Just seeing him there immediately brought me comfort.

In that moment, I knew the surgery was behind me, and I could begin focusing on healing.

Because my surgeon wanted to make sure I didn't develop a fever, I stayed overnight in the hospital for observation. I remember feeling relieved that the operation was over, even though I was understandably sore and tired.

One of my first complaints was about my surgical bra.

It felt incredibly tight.

I asked one of the nurses if there was any chance I could have a larger size. She smiled and explained that they hadn't wanted to change it immediately after surgery, but now that everything looked good, they would gladly bring me one that fit more comfortably.

As Robert helped me put it on, we both noticed that the bra had several small plastic rings attached near the bottom by short pieces of string.

We looked at each other.

"What are those for?"

Before either of us could ask the nurse, Robert grinned and said,

"I know—they're there so I can pull you in for a kiss."

We both burst out laughing.

Later we learned the rings were actually designed to hold drainage tubes if they became necessary.

Even in the middle of cancer treatment, Robert and I managed to find a reason to laugh.

Looking back, I'm grateful for moments like that.

Cancer brings plenty of serious conversations, difficult decisions, and anxious moments. Those unexpected bursts of humor don't make the cancer disappear, but they do make the journey a little lighter.

That simple joke reminded me that although cancer had become part of our lives, it hadn't taken away our ability to smile.

As I rested in my hospital room that evening, I found myself reflecting on everything that had happened over the past few weeks. Only a short time earlier, I had discovered a lump in my breast. Since then, life had become a whirlwind of tests, appointments, scans, consultations, and now surgery. It was all happening so quickly. Yet lying there in my hospital bed, I also felt something I hadn't expected.

Gratitude. Gratitude that the surgery was behind me. Gratitude for my skilled medical team. Gratitude for Robert sitting beside me. And gratitude that, despite everything, hope was still very much alive.

Although I didn't know what the pathology report would reveal or what treatments lay ahead, I had taken the first major step in my cancer journey.

One step was behind me.

The next would come when the time was right.

Recovery and Healing

Coming home from the hospital was both comforting and a little intimidating.

There is something reassuring about being surrounded by skilled nurses and doctors. Once you're home, however, you realize that your recovery is now in your own hands. Although I was happy to be sleeping in my own bed, I also knew I needed to give myself permission to heal.

Like many patients, I quickly discovered that recovery isn't something you can rush.

Our bodies have their own timetable.

One of the most important lessons I learned was to listen to my body. If I felt tired, I rested. If I needed help, I accepted it. Rather than expecting myself to bounce back immediately, I reminded myself that healing is a process, not an event.

Simple tasks that I normally took for granted suddenly required a little more thought. Reaching, lifting, and even getting dressed took patience. I learned to move a little more slowly and to celebrate the small victories that came with each passing day.

Every day I felt a little stronger than the day before.

Little by little, life began to feel normal again.

The Unexpected Side Effects

Before surgery, I thought my biggest challenge would be recovering from the incision itself.

Instead, I discovered there were a few surprises.

Because two sentinel lymph nodes were removed, I experienced numbness under my left arm. It felt strange at first, almost as though part of my body belonged to someone else. Although some sensation gradually returned over time, a degree of numbness has remained.

I also developed lymphedema, a condition caused by changes in the lymphatic system after lymph node removal and later affected by my radiation treatments. At first, I knew very little about lymphedema. Like many patients, I assumed that once my surgery healed, life would simply return to normal.

Instead, I found myself learning yet another new aspect of living after breast cancer.

Because lymphedema became such an important part of my journey, I've devoted an entire chapter to it later in this book. If you find yourself facing this challenge, I hope that chapter will reassure you that although lymphedema requires lifelong management, it doesn't prevent you from living a full, active, and meaningful life.

The Role of Hypnosis During Recovery

As a hypnosis instructor, people often ask whether I used hypnosis during my own recovery.

The answer is an enthusiastic **yes.**

Hypnosis became one of the most valuable tools I had available.

Each day, I would spend a few quiet minutes relaxing my body and focusing my mind on healing. Rather than dwelling on discomfort, I imagined my body doing exactly what it was designed to do—repairing tissues, reducing inflammation, strengthening my immune system, and becoming healthier with every passing day.

I also used hypnosis to help manage discomfort, reduce stress, sleep more comfortably, and remain patient with the healing process.

Perhaps the greatest benefit hypnosis gave me wasn't physical—it was emotional.

It reminded me that even though I couldn't control everything happening around me, I could always choose how I responded to it.

That realization gave me a sense of peace and control during a time when so much felt uncertain.

Throughout this book, I've shared many of the hypnosis techniques that helped me during my cancer journey. If hypnosis is new to you, I encourage you to approach it with an open mind. You don't need years of experience to benefit from it. Even a few minutes of focused relaxation each day can make a meaningful difference.

Looking Back

Looking back now, I realize that surgery marked far more than the removal of my cancer. It marked the beginning of learning to trust—trusting my surgeon and medical team, trusting my family and friends to support me, trusting my body to heal, and, perhaps most importantly, trusting myself. Surgery was the first major milestone in my treatment, but it wasn't the end of my journey. The pathology report showed that additional treatment would give me the best chance for a healthy future.

Like many breast cancer patients, my journey was just beginning.

Chemotherapy would become the next chapter.

At the time, the word **chemotherapy** filled me with fear. My imagination immediately pictured severe nausea, overwhelming fatigue, and losing my hair. I wondered how difficult it would be and whether I would be able to handle it.

As it turned out, chemotherapy wasn't exactly what I expected.

Yes, there were challenges.

There were difficult days.

But there were also unexpected moments of laughter, kindness, encouragement, and hope. Most importantly, I learned that the fear of chemotherapy was often worse than the treatment itself.

If chemotherapy is part of your treatment plan, I hope my experience will reassure you that while it may not be easy, it is manageable—and you don't have to face it alone.

A Few Final Thoughts

If you're preparing for surgery, remember that it's perfectly normal to feel anxious. Nearly everyone does. Ask your questions, follow your surgeon's instructions, and allow those who care about you to help.

Healing isn't measured only by the size of an incision or the date your stitches come out.

Healing happens physically, emotionally, and spiritually.

It happens one day at a time.

One deep breath at a time.

One act of kindness at a time.

Looking back, I no longer think of surgery as something I had to endure.

I think of it as the first step that allowed the rest of my treatment to do its job.

It was the beginning of removing the cancer...

and the beginning of discovering strengths I never knew I possessed.

As you continue reading, I'll share my experiences with chemotherapy—what frightened me beforehand, what actually happened during treatment, and the hypnosis techniques that helped me remain calm, comfortable, and hopeful every step of the way.

Self-Hypnosis Suggestions After Surgery

- Every breath I take brings me greater comfort, relaxation, and healing.
- My body knows exactly how to heal, and I allow that healing to happen naturally.
- Each day I become a little stronger, a little more comfortable, and a little more energetic.
- My incision is healing beautifully, one healthy cell at a time.
- Any discomfort I experience continues to lessen with every passing hour and every passing day.
- I remain calm, comfortable, and patient as my body recovers.
- I listen to my body and give it the rest it needs.
- I accept help from others, knowing that allowing myself to rest supports my healing.

- My medications are working exactly as they should to keep me comfortable and promote healing.
- Swelling continues to decrease as my body restores itself.
- My immune system is strong and supports my recovery.
- Every healthy choice I make nourishes my body and speeds my healing.
- I sleep peacefully, allowing my body to repair and restore itself.
- My energy returns a little more each day.
- I celebrate every small improvement because each one is a sign of healing.
- I trust the healing process and allow my body the time it needs.
- I remain hopeful, positive, and confident in my recovery.
- I focus on what I can do today, knowing tomorrow I will feel even stronger.
- I am grateful for the skilled professionals who cared for me and for my body's remarkable ability to heal.
- Each day I move one step closer to returning to the activities I enjoy.
- I am healing physically, emotionally, and mentally.
- My future is filled with hope, health, and new possibilities.
- **With every passing day, I notice small signs of progress. I trust my body's natural ability to heal. I am patient with myself, gentle with myself, and grateful for each step forward. Every day, in every way, I continue moving toward greater health, strength, and well-being.**

The **Control Room Technique** found in the Appendix can be used for any discomfort you may be experiencing

Chapter 7

Chemotherapy

Facing treatment with courage and hope

C**hemotherapy** works throughout the entire body. Think of it as a safety net. Even after surgery removes all visible cancer, a few microscopic cancer cells may have escaped into the bloodstream or lymphatic system. They are far too small to be seen on scans or during surgery. Chemotherapy travels throughout the body searching for and destroying these wandering cells before they have the chance to settle somewhere else and grow into new tumors. That is why chemotherapy is often recommended even when the surgeon believes all of the visible cancer has been removed.

When this photograph was taken, I wondered if I would ever feel like myself again. Today, I see not what cancer took from me, but the strength, resilience, and determination that carried me through one day at a time.

What Happens During a Typical Chemotherapy Session?

Before my first chemotherapy treatment, I had no idea what to expect. I pictured a frightening medical procedure with machines, alarms, and constant discomfort. The reality was much less intimidating than I had imagined.

When I arrived at the infusion center, I first checked in at the

reception desk. Before every treatment, a nurse took my vital signs, including my blood pressure, pulse, temperature, and weight. I also had blood drawn to make sure my white blood cell count and other blood counts were high enough for chemotherapy that day. My oncologist or physician assistant reviewed the results, asked how I had been feeling since my last treatment, discussed any side effects I was experiencing, and answered any questions before giving the approval to proceed.

Once everything looked good, I was escorted to the infusion room. It was a large room filled with comfortable reclining chairs where several patients received treatment at the same time. Although everyone was fighting a different battle, there was a quiet sense of camaraderie. We were all walking a similar path.

Several people had warned me that the infusion room could feel chilly, so I brought along a very special blanket. One of my former insurance clients, whom I had developed a wonderful long-distance friendship with over the years, lived in Alaska. When he learned I would be undergoing chemotherapy, he sent me a beautiful blanket covered with encouraging words. It wasn't just a blanket—it was a warm hug from a friend hundreds of miles away. Every time I wrapped myself in it, I was reminded that I was surrounded by people who cared.

After I settled into my chair, the nurse started my IV. Because my veins tended to roll, inserting the IV wasn't always easy. Fortunately, the infusion nurses were highly skilled, patient, and determined to make the process as comfortable as possible.

As they searched for a good vein, I naturally turned to one of the tools I had been teaching my hypnosis clients for years. I entered a relaxed state of self-hypnosis and focused on creating comfort in my arm. Rather than concentrating on the needle or the sensation of the IV being inserted, I directed my attention to feelings of calmness and relaxation. I imagined the area becoming comfortably numb, allowing me to remain peaceful while the nurses did their work. I found that self-hypnosis helped me stay relaxed, reduced my awareness of the discomfort, and made the entire process much easier.

Before receiving the chemotherapy drugs themselves, I was given medications to help prevent nausea and reduce the chance of an allergic reaction. These pre-medications are a routine part of many chemotherapy treatments and can make a significant difference in how you feel afterward.

Once the chemotherapy began, there was very little to do except relax. The medications flowed slowly through the IV tubing while the nurses checked on me regularly. They carefully monitored me for any signs of a reaction and were always available if I needed anything.

One thing that surprised me was how uneventful the infusion itself actually was. I didn't feel the chemotherapy working. There was no dramatic sensation. Mostly, I sat quietly, or lost myself in a good book.

In fact, I purposely saved one particular book just for my chemotherapy sessions—*Speak Ericksonian.* Since I have always enjoyed learning more about hypnosis, I looked forward to reading a little more with each treatment. It gave me something positive to anticipate and turned those long hours into an opportunity to continue growing professionally. Looking back, that book became an unexpected companion during my chemotherapy journey.

The hospital staff also did everything they could to make patients comfortable. Since my treatments began in the morning and lasted several hours, breakfast was provided—a yogurt, a muffin, and a fruit cup. Around lunchtime, I was offered a choice of a ham and cheese sandwich, chicken salad, tuna salad, or cheese, along with other light refreshments. These small acts of kindness helped make what could have been a very long day feel a little more like home.

When the infusion was finished, the IV was removed, and I was free to go home. The actual treatment session lasted several hours, but much of that time was simply waiting while the medications were infused safely.

As a hypnotist, I also used those hours to practice what I had taught my clients for decades. I entered a relaxed hypnotic state, used time distortion so the hours seemed to pass more quickly, and gave myself positive suggestions for calmness, comfort, and healing. Hypnosis didn't replace my medical treatment—it became another tool that helped me approach each chemotherapy session with greater confidence and peace.

For me, the hardest part wasn't sitting in the infusion chair. It was wondering how I would feel over the next several days. Everyone responds differently to chemotherapy. Some people experience only mild fatigue, while others have more significant side effects. Your oncology team will explain what to expect with your particular medications and, more importantly, what symptoms should prompt you to call the office.

Understanding the Side Effects of Chemotherapy

One of the first questions people ask after learning they need chemotherapy is, "How sick am I going to be?"

The honest answer is that everyone is different.

Some people experience only mild side effects, while others have a more difficult time. The type of chemotherapy you receive, your overall health, and even how your own body responds all play a role.

Chemotherapy works by destroying rapidly dividing cancer cells. Unfortunately, it cannot always distinguish between cancer cells and other healthy cells in your body that also divide quickly, such as those in your hair follicles, digestive tract, mouth, bone marrow, and nails. That's why side effects occur.

Fortunately, today's anti-nausea medications and supportive treatments have dramatically improved the chemotherapy experience for many patients. Many of the horror stories you may have heard from years ago simply are not the reality for most people today.

Some of the more common side effects include:

Fatigue: Fatigue is probably the most common side effect of chemotherapy. This isn't ordinary tiredness. It can feel like your body simply has less energy than usual. Learning to rest when needed and accepting help from others can make a tremendous difference.

Nausea: Years ago, nausea was one of the most feared aspects of chemotherapy. Fortunately, modern medications have greatly reduced this problem for many patients. My oncology team provided medications before treatment and prescriptions to use at home if needed.

Hair Loss: Not every chemotherapy drug causes hair loss, but many do. Losing your hair can be emotionally difficult because it is a visible reminder that you have cancer. Some people choose wigs, scarves, hats, or turbans, while others proudly go without covering their heads. There is no right or wrong choice—only what feels right for you.

Changes in Taste and Appetite: Foods you once enjoyed may suddenly taste different. Some people notice a metallic taste, while others lose interest in certain foods altogether. Eating smaller meals, staying hydrated, and experimenting with different foods often helps.

Lower Blood Counts: Chemotherapy can temporarily lower your white blood cells, red blood cells, and platelets. This may increase your risk of infection, leave you feeling more tired, or cause bruising more easily. Your blood counts are carefully monitored before every treatment to make sure it is safe to continue.

Mouth Sores: Some people develop tenderness or sores inside the mouth. Good oral hygiene and special mouth rinses recommended by your oncology team can often help prevent or relieve these symptoms.

Changes to Fingernails and Toenails: Some chemotherapy medications can cause nails to become brittle, discolored, or sensitive. These changes are usually temporary.

Peripheral Neuropathy: Certain chemotherapy drugs may cause numbness, tingling, or a "pins and needles" sensation in the hands or feet. Always report these symptoms to your oncology team, as adjustments to treatment may sometimes be necessary.

Chemo Brain: Many survivors describe temporary difficulty remembering words, concentrating, or multitasking. Often called "chemo brain," these changes usually improve with time.

What I Experienced Personally

Like everyone else receiving chemotherapy, I experienced some side effects, but thankfully they were manageable.

Fatigue was probably the most noticeable. There were days when I simply didn't have the energy I was used to. Rather than trying to push through it, Robert encouraged me to listen to my body and take a nap whenever I needed one. At first, that wasn't easy for me. I had always been someone who liked to stay busy, but I gradually learned that resting wasn't being lazy—it was an important part of healing.

Losing my hair was another milestone. About a week after my second chemotherapy treatment, I noticed strands of hair on my pillow when I woke up. Soon afterward, it began coming out in clumps—in the shower, on my hairbrush, and even on the furniture. Every handful was another reminder that I was a cancer patient.

I decided I wanted to shave it all off rather than watch it continue to fall out. Unfortunately, this was during the COVID-19 pandemic, when all the beauty salons and barber shops were closed.

So, Robert and I went out onto our deck, and he shaved my head.

When he finished, he looked at me, smiled, and said, "Now we're both bald!"

Robert normally keeps his head closely shaved. We often wear matching, color-coordinated outfits or matching funny cat T-shirts, so without missing a beat, he added, "Now we even have matching haircuts."

We both laughed.

That moment reminded me that cancer had not taken away our ability to find humor. Sometimes a good laugh really is one of the best medicines.

I also experienced a mild case of peripheral neuropathy in the toes of my right foot. It felt like pins and needles, but fortunately it never became severe. I had some nausea as well, but thanks to the medications my oncology team prescribed—and the relaxation and hypnosis techniques I practiced—it remained mild and manageable.

Looking back, I realize that my fear before the first chemotherapy treatment was much greater than the treatment itself. Once I knew what to expect, each session became a little less intimidating. The unknown had become familiar, and with every treatment I completed, I knew I was one step closer to the finish line.

Throughout my chemotherapy, I learned to take one day at a time. Rather than worrying about everything that might happen tomorrow, I focused on what was happening today. If I experienced a side effect, I talked with my oncology team, and together we found ways to manage it. Although chemotherapy certainly had its challenges, I was fortunate that my side effects were manageable and not nearly as overwhelming as I had imagined.

There is one message I especially want you to remember if chemotherapy is part of your journey: it is temporary. Every infusion you complete is one treatment behind you and one treatment closer to hearing those wonderful words, "Your chemotherapy is finished."

When I look back on those months, I don't remember the IVs, the medications, or even the long hours spent in the infusion chair. I remember the kindness of the nurses, the warmth of a blanket sent by a thoughtful friend in Alaska, the pages of a book that reminded me that life—and learning—continued, even during cancer treatment, and the unwavering love and support of Robert. Those simple moments carried me through one treatment at a time.

The day I rang the cancer bell wasn't simply the end of chemotherapy. It was a celebration of perseverance, hope, and the realization that I was stronger than I had ever imagined. Looking back now, I understand that chemotherapy wasn't just something I endured—it was one more step on my journey toward healing.

Using Self-Hypnosis During Chemotherapy

Chemotherapy can sometimes bring feelings of uncertainty, anxiety, or simply the challenge of sitting through a long infusion. I found that self-hypnosis helped me relax, remain calm, and feel more comfortable throughout my treatments. It also helped the hours seem to pass much more quickly.

While self-hypnosis is not a substitute for your chemotherapy medications or your oncology team's care, it can become another valuable tool to help you feel more peaceful, comfortable, and in control.

For a brief emotional reset before or during treatment, use the **Self-Hypnosis Suggestion Exercise** found in the Appendix and repeat a few of the suggestions below. When you have more time, begin with the **Progressive Relaxation Exercise**, and include as many of these suggestions as you need.

Self-Hypnosis Suggestions for Chemotherapy

Before the IV Is Inserted

- As the nurse prepares my IV, I remain calm, relaxed, and comfortable.
- My arm feels pleasantly heavy, comfortably numb, and completely at ease as the IV is inserted.
- I focus on my breathing and allow any brief discomfort to fade quickly into the background.
- I direct my attention to feelings of comfort and relaxation, allowing my body to cooperate easily with the procedure.
- Each breath helps me relax more deeply, making the IV insertion easier and more comfortable than I imagined.

During the Infusion

- With every slow, comfortable breath, I become more relaxed and peaceful.
- I feel calm, safe, and confident throughout my treatment.
- My body accepts this treatment as an important step toward healing.
- The medications are doing exactly what they are designed to do—helping my body fight cancer.

- I remain comfortable, relaxed, and in control throughout my infusion.
- The nurses and medical team are caring for me with skill, compassion, and expertise.
- Time seems to pass pleasantly and quickly. Before I know it, today's treatment will be complete.
- Every minute that passes brings me closer to the end of today's infusion.
- The hours seem to drift by as though only minutes have passed.
- My mind remains peaceful while my body receives the treatment it needs.
- I easily release fear, worry, and tension with each exhale.

Healing and Recovery

- I welcome feelings of comfort, hope, and confidence.
- I trust my body's ability to recover and heal.
- Every treatment I complete brings me one step closer to the finish line.
- I am stronger than I sometimes realize.
- One treatment at a time. One day at a time. One step at a time.
- Each session is another step toward health, healing, and my own rainbow after the storm.

As I repeated these suggestions, I often opened my book, settled under my special blanket from my friend, and before I knew it, the nurses were telling me my treatment was finished.

When your chemotherapy session is over, take a moment to acknowledge what you've accomplished. Every infusion you complete is one treatment behind you and one treatment closer to recovery. Give yourself credit for your courage, your perseverance, and your commitment to healing.

Every treatment brings me closer to healing. I trust the journey, I embrace hope, and I know that after every storm comes the possibility of a rainbow.

Chapter 8

Radiation

One Step Closer to the Finish Line

After completing chemotherapy, I thought the hardest part of my treatment was behind me. I had made it through surgery, four rounds of chemotherapy, and all of the emotions that came with them. Surely, I was nearing the finish line.

Not quite.

My oncologist explained that the next step would be radiation therapy. Although I had heard of radiation, I really didn't know what to expect. Like many people, I imagined large machines, frightening equipment, and unpleasant side effects. Once again, I found myself stepping into unfamiliar territory.

As it turned out, radiation was very different from chemotherapy.

Unlike chemotherapy, which travels throughout the body, radiation is a local treatment. It uses carefully targeted, high-energy beams to destroy cancer cells that may remain in one specific area after surgery. Even when a surgeon removes every visible sign of cancer, microscopic cancer cells can sometimes remain behind. Radiation helps destroy those remaining cells and reduces the chance that the cancer will return.

I often explain the difference this way. If chemotherapy is like installing a whole-house security system, radiation is like adding an extra lock to the front door. Both are designed to protect you, but they work in different ways.

Many people are surprised to learn that radiation treatments themselves are painless. You don't feel the radiation while it is being delivered. The actual treatment usually lasts only a few minutes, although getting into the correct position often takes longer than the treatment itself. Most patients receive treatments Monday through Friday for several weeks, depending on their diagnosis and treatment plan.

Like chemotherapy, radiation can cause side effects. These vary from person to person and depend on the area being treated. Some people experience only mild side effects, while others find treatment more challenging. Knowing what to expect helped me feel less anxious. The more I understood about the process, the less frightening it became.

Why I Needed Radiation

Even though my surgeon had successfully removed my tumors and I had completed chemotherapy, my treatment wasn't quite finished. My oncologist recommended radiation therapy to destroy any microscopic cancer cells that might still remain in my breast and surrounding tissues. This additional treatment would further reduce the risk of the cancer returning.

I'll admit, my first thought was, *Haven't I already been through enough?*

But as my doctors carefully explained the purpose of radiation, I realized this wasn't because my previous treatments hadn't worked. It was another layer of protection—another important step toward giving me the best possible chance for a healthy future.

Cancer treatment is often built one step upon another. Surgery removed the visible cancer. Chemotherapy traveled throughout my body to destroy cancer cells that might have escaped. Radiation would now focus on the area where the cancer had begun. Each treatment had a different purpose, and together they formed a complete plan.

Meeting My Radiation Oncologist

My first appointment with the radiation oncologist was very different from my visits with my surgeon and medical oncologist. We talked about why radiation was recommended, what area would be treated, how many treatments I would need, what side effects I might experience, and how my progress would be monitored.

I quickly learned that radiation therapy is not a one-size-fits-all treatment. Every patient's treatment plan is carefully designed specifically for them. The location of the cancer, the type of cancer, previous treatments, and many other factors are all taken into consideration before the first treatment ever begins.

That personalized approach gave me confidence. I knew my treatment plan had been designed just for me.

The Simulation

Before my first radiation treatment, I had what is called a **simulation.** Despite its name, there was nothing imaginary about it. This planning appointment allowed the radiation team to map out exactly where the radiation beams would be directed.

During the simulation, I lay on the treatment table while a CT scan was performed. The therapists carefully positioned my body so that I could be placed in exactly the same position every day throughout my treatments. Tiny tattoo marks were placed on my skin to serve as permanent reference points, helping the therapists align the radiation with remarkable precision.

Although the simulation appointment took longer than an actual treatment session, it was one of the most important parts of the entire process. Every measurement, every mark, and every adjustment helped ensure that the radiation would be delivered accurately while protecting as much healthy tissue as possible.

Once the planning was complete, I was ready to begin my daily treatments.

My Daily Treatments

Once my treatments began, radiation quickly became part of my daily routine. Monday through Friday, for five weeks, I made the short drive to the treatment center. Before long, it became just another part of my day—one more step toward healing.

The treatment itself was surprisingly quick. Most of each appointment was actually spent getting me into the exact position needed for the radiation. Precision was everything. Once I was perfectly aligned, the therapists left the room, but they could see and hear me the entire time through cameras and an intercom.

Because even the slightest movement could affect the accuracy of the treatment, it was important that I remain completely still. Fortunately, one of the fascinating phenomena of hypnosis, called **catalepsy**, made that much easier.

Catalepsy is a natural hypnotic state in which a part of the body can remain comfortably still in whatever position it has been placed, without strain or discomfort. Before each treatment, I quietly used self-hypnosis, allowing my body to become relaxed, steady, and comfortably motionless. Rather than feeling stiff or tense, I felt calm and completely at ease. Remaining still became surprisingly easy, and I later found myself using this same technique during MRIs, X-rays, bone density scans, and other medical tests that required me to hold one position for several minutes.

One of the radiation therapists always asked what kind of music I would like to listen to while the machine did its work. My answer was always the same.

"The '60s, please."

I've always loved the music of that era. Then, with a smile, I would add, "Just make sure you don't play any dance music, or I'll be tempted to jump off the table and start dancing."

One day, after they had carefully positioned me and reminded me to remain perfectly still, the music began. Of all the songs they could have chosen, I heard *Do You Love Me* by The Contours. I couldn't help but smile to myself. All I could think about was jumping off the table and doing the Stroll.

Of course, I stayed exactly where I was. Thanks to self-hypnosis—and a little self-control—I remained perfectly still while silently enjoying the music. It reminded me that even in the middle of cancer treatment, there was still room for laughter, fond memories, and a great old song.

As the machine slowly moved around me, delivering the radiation from different angles, I felt absolutely nothing. There was no pain, no heat, and no sensation at all. Within just a few minutes, the treatment was finished, and I was on my way home.

As the days passed, the radiation therapists became familiar faces. Their kindness, encouragement, and cheerful smiles made each visit a little easier. They understood that, although the treatments were routine for them, each patient walking through their doors was facing one of the most challenging experiences of their life. Their compassion made all the difference, and I genuinely looked forward to seeing them each day.

The Side Effects

Like chemotherapy, radiation has side effects, but they are usually quite different. Not everyone experiences the same side effects, and some people have very few. Knowing what might happen helped me feel prepared rather than surprised.

For many people, the most common side effect is fatigue. It isn't simply feeling sleepy. It can feel like your body is working overtime as it repairs healthy tissue while responding to the treatment. I learned to listen to my body. On days when I needed to rest, I rested without feeling guilty.

The skin in the treated area often changes gradually as treatment continues. It may become red, dry, itchy, tender, or darker in color—much like a sunburn. Because my radiation was directed to my left breast, those were the changes I experienced. As the weeks passed, my breast became noticeably darker.

One day, one of the radiation therapists commented on how much my skin had darkened. Never wanting to miss an opportunity for a little humor, I smiled and said, "Now I have to get my breasts to match. I guess I'll have to lie out in the sun and tan the right one."

We both laughed.

Laughter didn't change the side effects, but it certainly made them easier to live with.

Fortunately, my radiation team monitored my skin closely throughout treatment and gave me suggestions for keeping it as comfortable as possible. I followed their recommendations, wore loose, comfortable clothing, and tried to be patient with my body's healing process.

Everyone's experience with radiation is different. Some people notice only mild changes, while others experience more discomfort. Whatever your experience, don't hesitate to tell your radiation team about any concerns you have. They have many ways to help manage side effects and keep you as comfortable as possible throughout treatment.

A Treatment Decision

As my radiation treatments progressed, my doctors began discussing whether I should receive what is called a **radiation boost**—a few additional treatments directed specifically at the area where the tumor had been removed. The purpose of the boost is to provide an extra layer of protection by treating the area where cancer is most likely to recur.

By that time, however, I had already developed breast lymphedema. My breast had become swollen with fluid, and my medical team was concerned that the additional radiation could make the swelling even worse.

I vividly remember lying on the treatment table, wearing nothing from the waist up, while four or five physicians and radiation therapists gathered around discussing my situation. They were carefully weighing the benefits of the radiation boost against the possibility of increasing my lymphedema.

It was a little awkward lying there while everyone talked about me as though I wasn't even in the room.

Trying to lighten the moment—as I often did throughout my cancer journey—I smiled and said,

"If I'd known I was going to have an audience, I would have sold tickets."

The room erupted in laughter.

In the end, my radiation oncologist and the rest of my medical team decided that the potential benefits of the boost did not outweigh the increased risk of making my lymphedema worse. Although I was disappointed, I understood they were making the best decision for me.

That experience reminded me that cancer treatment isn't always straightforward. Sometimes there isn't a single "right" answer. Medical decisions are often made by carefully balancing the benefits and the risks, and every treatment plan must be individualized because every patient is unique.

Little did I know that lymphedema would eventually become its own chapter in my cancer journey.

Taking Care of Myself

One of the most important lessons I learned during radiation was to listen to my body.

When I felt tired, I rested.

I stayed well hydrated, ate nutritious foods, followed my radiation team's recommendations for skin care, and wore loose, comfortable clothing whenever possible. I also accepted help when I needed it—something that didn't always come naturally to me but became one of the greatest lessons cancer taught me.

Just as importantly, I continued using self-hypnosis before each treatment. Instead of focusing on fear or worrying about side effects, I focused on healing. I imagined the radiation doing exactly what it had been designed to do—destroying any remaining cancer cells while allowing my healthy cells to recover and heal.

Those few quiet minutes before each treatment helped me feel calmer, more comfortable, and more in control. They reminded me that even when I couldn't control everything happening around me, I could always influence how I responded.

Ringing the Bell

Finally, the day arrived for my last radiation treatment.

Like many cancer centers, mine had a bell that patients ring to celebrate the completion of treatment. As I reached for the rope and heard the bell ring, I was overwhelmed with gratitude, relief, pride, and hope.

I had done it.

The journey hadn't been easy. Surgery, chemotherapy, radiation, and recovery had tested me in ways I never could have imagined. There had been fear, uncertainty, tears, laughter, setbacks, and victories.

Standing there that day, I realized just how far I had come.

The bell didn't mean my journey was over. There would still be follow-up appointments, hormone therapy, and the challenges of living with lymphedema. But it marked the end of one very important chapter and the beginning of another.

Looking Back

Looking back now, radiation was not nearly as frightening as I had imagined it would be. As with so many parts of my cancer journey, the anticipation was often worse than the treatment itself.

Each appointment became one smaller step toward healing. Day after day, treatment after treatment, I moved closer to recovery.

Cancer taught me that healing rarely happens all at once. It happens one appointment, one treatment, one day, and one hopeful step at a time.

Radiation was one of those steps.

Completing it brought me one step closer to closing that chapter of my life and moving forward with hope, gratitude, and a deeper appreciation for every ordinary day.

Self-Hypnosis Suggestions

For Radiation Treatments

- Each radiation treatment is helping my body heal.
- I remain calm, comfortable, and relaxed throughout every session.
- My body accepts this treatment easily and safely.
- The radiation is doing exactly what it is designed to do.
- Healthy cells recover quickly while unhealthy cells are eliminated.
- Every treatment brings me one step closer to recovery.
- I feel grateful for the skilled professionals caring for me.
- My body grows stronger with each passing day.
- I look forward with hope and confidence.
- Every treatment brings me closer to ringing the bell.

For Remaining Still During Medical Procedures

- My body is comfortably relaxed, steady, and perfectly still.
- Every muscle knows exactly how to remain calm and motionless.
- Remaining still feels natural, easy, and comfortable.
- My breathing is slow, gentle, and relaxed while the rest of my body remains quiet.
- I am completely comfortable in this position.
- My body remains exactly where it needs to be until the procedure is complete.
- Each passing moment seems shorter than the one before.
- I feel peaceful, patient, and completely at ease.
- My mind is calm while my body remains comfortably still.

- Every moment of stillness is helping my healthcare team provide the very best care.
- I remain relaxed, confident, and in control throughout this procedure.
- Before I know it, the procedure will be finished, and I will have done exactly what my body needed to do.

Chapter 9

My Journey with Lymphedema

Before I share my own experience, it may be helpful to understand what lymphedema is.

Lymphedema is swelling that occurs when lymph fluid builds up because the lymphatic system is no longer able to drain that fluid efficiently. Think of the lymphatic system as your body's natural drainage network. It is made up of tiny vessels and lymph nodes that help remove excess fluid, filter waste products, and carry infection-fighting cells throughout the body.

For many breast cancer patients, lymphedema can develop after surgery or radiation treatment, particularly if lymph nodes have been removed or damaged. It most commonly affects the arm, hand, breast, or chest on the side where treatment was received, although it can occur in other areas as well.

Some people develop lymphedema shortly after treatment, while others may not notice symptoms until months—or even years—later. Not everyone who has lymph nodes removed will develop lymphedema, but recognizing the early signs is important because prompt treatment can often keep it from becoming more severe.

The good news is that lymphedema can usually be managed very successfully. With proper treatment, healthy habits, and ongoing self-care, many people continue to lead active, fulfilling lives while keeping their symptoms well under control.

Unfortunately, I discovered firsthand that even when you do everything you're supposed to do, lymphedema can still happen.

My first experience with lymphedema actually began shortly after my breast surgery.

Following surgery, my breast became swollen with fluid that was diagnosed as lymphedema. The swelling remained throughout chemotherapy and radiation treatments. Near the end of my radiation therapy, my radiation oncologist wanted to give me what is called a **"boost"**—an additional dose of radiation directed at the area where the cancer had been removed to further reduce the risk of recurrence.

I vividly remember lying on the treatment table, wearing nothing from the waist up, while four or five physicians and technicians gathered around discussing whether the swelling would prevent the boost from being effective. It was a little embarrassing lying there while everyone talked about me as though I wasn't even in the room.

Trying to lighten the moment—as I often did throughout my cancer journey—I smiled and said,

"If I'd known I was going to have an audience, I would have sold tickets."

The room erupted in laughter.

In the end, they decided not to give the boost because the swelling would interfere with accurately targeting the treatment. Although I was disappointed, I understood they were making the best medical decision for me.

My oncologist referred me to a physical therapist specially trained in treating lymphedema. Through manual lymph drainage massage, she was able to gradually move the excess fluid away from my breast, and eventually the swelling resolved.

I thought that chapter of my life had closed.

I was wrong.

Years later, I developed lymphedema again—this time in my left arm and hand.

That diagnosis was one of the biggest emotional challenges I faced after cancer.

I was devastated.

I remember my oncologist telling me to avoid blood draws, injections, and blood pressure readings in my left arm after surgery. I followed those instructions faithfully, always using my right arm whenever possible. What I don't remember is anyone explaining exactly why those precautions were so important or that, despite being careful, lymphedema could still develop years later.

My physical therapist explained that I would also need to protect my arm from cuts, scratches, burns, insect bites, and sunburn. Since we had a cat, avoiding scratches wasn't always easy! She also stressed the importance of preventing infection and taking good care of my skin.

Even though I did my best to follow every recommendation, lymphedema developed anyway.

When I first noticed swelling in my left arm and hand, I contacted my oncologist immediately. After examining me, she confirmed what I had feared and referred me to a certified lymphedema physical therapist.

The swelling involved my upper arm, lower arm, and hand, although thankfully not my fingertips. My therapist carefully measured my arm and began treatment right away.

For the next two months, I went to physical therapy every Monday, Wednesday, and Friday. Each visit followed the same routine. My therapist removed the compression bandages, performed manual lymph drainage massage, and then carefully rewrapped my arm before I left.

The bandages were so bulky that I couldn't fit my arm into the sleeve of my winter coat. Since it was February and bitterly cold outside, I had to buy a sleeveless cape and a heavy shawl instead. They kept me covered, but they certainly didn't keep me as warm.

Even taking a shower became complicated. I had to wear a waterproof sleeve to protect the bandages, and I couldn't put it on or take it off by myself.

Thankfully, I wasn't alone.

Robert patiently helped me every day. Even members of my dental office and my OB/GYN's office cheerfully pitched in whenever I had appointments.

One memory still makes me smile.

My son had taken me out to breakfast, and afterward he helped me put on my shawl and cape before we left the restaurant. As I looked up, I noticed an elderly couple sitting in the next booth smiling from ear to ear. Their expressions seemed to say, *"Isn't that wonderful to see a son taking such loving care of his mother?"*

It was one of those quiet moments that reminded me how much love surrounded me during that difficult time.

After about six weeks, the swelling had improved enough for me to be fitted for permanent compression garments—a daytime sleeve and glove, along with a nighttime sleeve and glove that I would wear for the rest of my life.

Those words...

"for the rest of my life"...

were hard to hear.

This wasn't a temporary side effect.

It was my new normal.

My physical therapist taught me how to perform manual lymph drainage on myself, and she also taught Robert how to massage the different lymphatic pathways to encourage healthy drainage. Once again, we became a team.

Physically, I was learning how to manage lymphedema.

Emotionally, however, I still had work to do.

Every time I looked at my compression garments, they reminded me that cancer had left me with a permanent reminder of everything I had been through.

That was when Robert, not only as my husband but also as a hypnotist, gently helped me change my perspective.

Through hypnosis, I gradually stopped thinking of my compression garments as something I *had* to wear and began seeing them as one more tool that was helping me stay healthy.

Instead of feeling resentment each time I put them on, I began feeling gratitude that I had something that could help manage my condition.

Acceptance didn't mean I liked having lymphedema.

It meant I stopped allowing it to define me.

The garments became no different than eating healthy foods, staying active, or keeping my follow-up appointments. They simply became another way of taking care of myself.

Looking back now, I realize that lymphedema changed many of my daily routines, but it never changed who I was. It taught me that healing is about more than recovering physically. Sometimes healing means learning to adapt, accepting what cannot be changed, appreciating the people who walk beside you, and continuing to move forward with hope.

That, perhaps, is one of the greatest lessons cancer taught me.

As part of my physical therapy, Nancy, my lymphedema therapist, spent several sessions teaching me how to properly put on and remove both my daytime compression sleeve and glove and my nighttime compression garment. At first, it wasn't easy. The garments fit so snugly that getting them on correctly could be quite a challenge.

Nancy showed me several tricks that made the process much easier. One was to wear a surgical glove, which provided just enough tackiness to help grip and pull the compression garment into place. She also suggested trying a garden glove. After using both, I found that the garden glove worked best. Its textured surface gave me a much better grip, making it much easier to pull the garment on without struggling.

It was such a simple, inexpensive suggestion, but it made a world of difference. That experience taught me that living with lymphedema is often about discovering little tips and techniques that make everyday life easier. Over time, I collected several of those practical hints, and I'd like to share them with you in the hope that they make your journey a little easier, too.

If you're having difficulty putting on your compression garment, ask your lymphedema therapist to demonstrate different techniques and recommend helpful tools. Sometimes a simple suggestion can make a world of difference.

Everyday Tips for Living with Lymphedema

When you have lymphedema, even small cuts, burns, or insect bites can increase your risk of infection. Over time, I learned that a few simple habits became part of my daily routine. They soon became second nature.

Here are some of the things that have helped me:

- **Wear gardening gloves** whenever you're working in the yard to protect your hands from cuts, thorns, and insect bites. (I don't garden, but if you do…)
- **Wear rubber or dishwashing gloves** when washing dishes or using household cleaning products.
- **Use disposable plastic food-preparation gloves** when handling raw meat, poultry, or fish to reduce the risk of bacteria entering even tiny cuts on your hands. I

even wear these while I'm eating to prevent the garment from being soiled with food.

- **Moisturize your skin daily** to help prevent dry, cracked skin.
- **Protect your skin from the sun** by using sunscreen and avoiding sunburn.
- **Use insect repellent** when spending time outdoors.
- **Be careful when trimming your nails.** Avoid cutting your cuticles, and consider having a professional manicure only if the salon follows excellent sanitation practices.
- **Wear gloves for household chores** that could cause scrapes or blisters.
- **Avoid carrying heavy bags** on the affected arm whenever possible.
- **Avoid having blood pressure taken, blood drawn, injections, or IVs** in the affected arm unless there is no other reasonable option.
- **Wear your compression sleeve and glove as recommended** by your lymphedema therapist.
- **Perform your prescribed exercises and lymphatic massage** as instructed.
- **Watch for signs of infection,** such as increased redness, warmth, swelling, fever, or pain, and contact your healthcare provider promptly if they occur.
- **Don't ignore changes.** Early treatment of swelling is much easier than waiting until it becomes more severe.

Living with lymphedema requires a few extra precautions, but it doesn't have to prevent you from enjoying life. These simple habits have allowed me to continue gardening, traveling, cooking, and doing the things I love. Rather than seeing them as restrictions, I came to think of them as small acts of self-care—daily reminders that my body deserves kindness and protection.

Hypnosis Suggestions for Managing Lymphedema

One of the greatest blessings during my recovery was having Robert by my side. He helped me in very practical ways—putting on my nighttime garment, learning manual lymph drainage massage, and encouraging me on the days when I felt discouraged.

But he also helped care for something that couldn't be measured with a tape measure.

He helped care for my mind.

I was fortunate that Robert could help care for both my body and my mind.

While hypnosis is **not** a cure for lymphedema, I found it to be a valuable tool for managing the emotional side of living with a chronic condition. It helped me feel calmer, less frustrated, and more accepting of what had become my new normal. As my body relaxed, I often noticed that I felt more comfortable, and I became more focused on what I *could* do rather than what I had lost.

One of the things I appreciate most about hypnosis is that it works alongside—not instead of—good medical care. It can complement the treatment plan recommended by your healthcare team by helping reduce stress, easing muscular tension, encouraging healthy self-care habits, and creating a greater sense of control.

When we become anxious or fearful, our bodies naturally tense. We may hold our breath, tighten our muscles, and focus on every sensation. While those reactions are completely understandable, they can leave us feeling even more uncomfortable. Relaxation helps interrupt that cycle.

During hypnosis, I often imagined my lymphatic system working in harmony with my treatment. I pictured the lymphatic vessels gently opening, allowing lymph fluid to move comfortably through the pathways and eventually return to the bloodstream, where my body could process it naturally. Whether you picture a peaceful stream, a beautiful garden irrigation system, or the gentle rhythm of the ocean tide, these calming images can help create a greater sense of cooperation between your mind and your body.

Although visualization cannot remove lymphedema, many people find that it helps them feel calmer, more hopeful, and more engaged in their own healing journey.

The following suggestions and visualizations are examples of imagery that you may find helpful as you practice self-hypnosis or simply take a few quiet moments each day to relax and reconnect with your body's remarkable ability to heal, adapt, and restore balance.

Self Hypnosis Suggestions

- "Your body is learning balance and comfort more and more each day."
- "You become increasingly aware of healthy sensations."
- "You listen to your body calmly and respond with confidence."
- "Each breath encourages relaxation and healthy circulation throughout your body."
- "You allow your arm and body to feel lighter, calmer, and more comfortable."

- "You easily remember to care for your body in healthy, supportive ways."
- "You trust yourself to notice changes early and respond appropriately."
- "Your mind and body work together to support healing and comfort."

Visualization

You may imagine a peaceful flowing stream moving gently and continuously, carrying away excess fluid with ease and comfort. Or you may picture the lymphatic system as a network of calm flowing pathways opening and clearing naturally, allowing your body to restore balance and movement.

Some people find it comforting to imagine warmth, softness, and lightness moving through the affected area, bringing relaxation and ease with every breath.

Self-Hypnosis Reinforcement

During self-hypnosis, patients may repeat:

"I remain calm, aware, and confident.

My body continues to support balance, comfort, and healthy flow."

From this day forward, each time you see your compression garment, touch it, or put it on, you may automatically pause for just a moment...take one slow, comfortable breath...and smile to yourself, knowing:

"This is one more way I care for myself."

And that simple thought can make putting it on feel easier...more automatic...and more positive each day.

See the Appendix for a Compression Garment Acceptance script.

Affirmation

"I care for my body with patience, calmness, and confidence."

Self-Hypnosis Practice

Spend several minutes each day focusing on slow breathing while imagining healthy circulation and comfortable movement flowing naturally throughout your body.

Lymphedema can feel frustrating and discouraging at times, but many people learn to manage it successfully. Early attention, gentle self-care, movement, and emotional calmness can all make a meaningful difference.

Also See

Appendix C The Garden Gate Technique and

Appendix D Compression Garment Acceptance

Chapter 10

Why Hypnosis?

Using the power of the Mind

Many people have misconceptions about hypnosis because of what they have seen in movies or stage shows. In reality, hypnosis is simply a natural state of focused attention and deep relaxation. It is much like becoming completely absorbed in a good book or movie, where you lose track of time and become less aware of everything happening around you.

During hypnosis, you remain awake, aware, and in control. You cannot be made to do anything against your values or wishes. Instead, hypnosis helps quiet the constant chatter of the conscious mind, allowing helpful suggestions to be accepted more easily.

For people facing cancer, hypnosis can be a valuable tool for reducing anxiety, managing pain, improving sleep, easing treatment-related stress, and fostering a greater sense of calm and control. While hypnosis does **not** treat or cure cancer, research has shown that it can help reduce many of the physical and emotional challenges that often accompany diagnosis and treatment.

Think of hypnosis as a way of tapping into your mind's natural ability to help your body relax, cope, and heal emotionally. It is another tool—alongside your medical care—that can help you navigate your cancer journey with greater comfort, confidence, and resilience.

How to Use the Self-Hypnosis Scripts

The appendices contain a collection of self-hypnosis scripts that you can use whenever you need them. Each script is designed to help you cope with a different aspect of your cancer journey—from reducing stress and managing fear to improving sleep, increasing comfort, and strengthening hope.

The **Progressive Relaxation** exercise is the starting point for the long scripts in the Appendix. Think of it as the doorway into hypnosis. It helps you relax your body, quiet your mind, and enter a comfortable state of focused attention where the suggestions that follow can become more meaningful and effective. Each time you use one of the self-hypnosis scripts, begin with the Progressive Relaxation exercise.

Once you are comfortably in hypnosis, you have several options. You may ask a trusted friend, family member, or caregiver to slowly read the script to you. You may gently open your eyes—yes, you really can open your eyes and remain in hypnosis—and read the script yourself. Or you may record the script in your own voice and listen to the recording whenever you wish.

Using the **Self Hypnosis Suggestion** script

Throughout this book, you'll find brief self-hypnosis suggestions at the end of many chapters. These are designed for those moments when you need a quick emotional reset but don't have time to complete one of the longer self-hypnosis exercises in the Appendix. Think of them as "mini hypnosis sessions" that can be done in just a few minutes. From the selection offered, pick 2 or 3 suggestions that apply to you in the moment. Insert those in the section … *Pause here and slowly*

To use these suggestions, begin with the **Self-Hypnosis Suggestion** exercise listed in the Appendix. This short exercise helps you relax, focus your attention, and prepare your mind to accept positive suggestions. When you reach the point in the script that says,

"Pause here and slowly repeat the self-hypnosis suggestions from the chapter you are working on. Continue repeating them until they feel natural and meaningful to you. Then continue with the remainder of the exercise.,"

simply replace those words with the chosen two or three brief suggestions provided at the end of the chapter you are reading. Repeat the suggestions slowly, allowing yourself to fully absorb their meaning before continuing to the end of the exercise.

Whether you use these brief self-hypnosis suggestions exercises or the longer scripts in the Appendix, remember there is no perfect way to practice self-hypnosis. Even spending just a few minutes calming your mind, relaxing your body, and focusing on positive, healing thoughts can help reduce stress, strengthen your sense of control, and support your emotional well-being throughout your cancer journey.

Many people are surprised to learn that hypnosis is not sleep. Rather, it is a natural state of focused attention and relaxed awareness. Simply choose the method that feels most comfortable for you. There is no "right" or "wrong" way to use these exercises. The goal is to relax, absorb the positive suggestions, and allow your mind and body to work together in support of your healing, comfort, and overall well-being.

In Brief

For the Progressive Relaxation Exercise

Allow **20–30 minutes**. Begin by using the Progressive Relaxation exercise to guide yourself into hypnosis. Once you are comfortably in hypnosis, continue with the script from the Appendix list that best meets your needs. Choose the method that works best for you:

- Ask someone you trust to slowly read the script aloud.
- Record the script in your own voice and play it back.
- Enter hypnosis using the Progressive Relaxation exercise, then gently open your eyes and read the script yourself while remaining in hypnosis.

For the Self-Hypnosis Suggestion Exercise

Allow **3–5 minutes**. Use this exercise whenever you need a quick emotional reset or don't have time for a longer self-hypnosis session.

- Begin with the Self-Hypnosis Suggestion exercise in the Appendix.
- When you reach the instruction that says, *"Pause here and slowly repeat the self-hypnosis suggestions from the chapter you are working on,"* use the brief suggestions provided at the end of the chapter you are reading.
- Repeat the suggestions slowly and thoughtfully, allowing yourself to absorb their meaning before completing the exercise.

- Complete the exercise by counting yourself out of hypnosis as directed.
- Practice this exercise as often as needed throughout the day to reinforce positive thoughts, reduce stress, and strengthen your sense of calm and control.

Remember, these exercises are not about doing hypnosis perfectly. They are simply tools to help you relax, quiet your mind, and tap into your own inner resources for healing. The more often you practice, the more natural and effective the process is likely to become.

Whether you have five minutes or thirty, I encourage you to make self-hypnosis a regular part of your self-care routine. Like any skill, it becomes easier and more effective with practice. Whenever you need a little extra support, simply turn to the Appendix and choose the exercise that best meets your needs.

You don't have to wait until you're feeling overwhelmed to use self-hypnosis. In fact, you'll often receive the greatest benefit when you practice it regularly. Just a few minutes each day can help you feel calmer, more relaxed, and better prepared to handle whatever comes your way.

A few words of caution: Do not practice these exercises when you are overly tired, as you may simply drift off to sleep before receiving the full benefit of the suggestions. If you record the scripts in your own voice, never listen to them while driving, operating machinery, or engaging in any activity that requires your full attention. Instead, use them only when you can relax safely and without interruption.

Chapter 11

Coping with Fear, Uncertainty, and the "What Ifs"

Managing Anxiety, Waiting, and Fear of Recurrence

Even as I made meaningful lifestyle changes and began to regain a sense of control over my health, I discovered that another challenge quietly remained—learning how to live with uncertainty. There were moments between scans, appointments, and follow-ups when fear would surface uninvited, bringing with it the familiar "what ifs" that could easily take over my thoughts. What if the cancer returns? What if something has been missed? It was in these moments that I realized healing was not only physical, but deeply emotional as well. I began to understand that I needed tools not just for my body, but for my mind—ways to steady myself, calm the internal noise, and create a sense of safety even when nothing around me had changed. This became the space where deeper hypnosis work truly began to matter.

The "What If" Mind

One of the things that surprised me most after my treatment ended was how quickly my mind could jump to the worst possible conclusion. During treatment, there was always another appointment, another blood test, another chemotherapy session, or another visit with my oncologist. My medical team was watching me closely, and I knew exactly what came next. When treatment ended, however, life became quieter. While I had looked forward to that day, the silence sometimes left room for fear to creep in. A slight ache, a headache, feeling unusually tired, or a swollen lymph node after a cold could quickly send my thoughts racing. *What if it's back? What if they missed something? What if I'm starting this journey all over again?* I eventually realized that my mind wasn't trying to frighten me—it was trying to protect me. After living through something as life-changing as cancer, my brain had become extra alert to anything that might signal danger. The challenge was that a mind constantly searching for danger often finds it, even when it isn't really there. Learning to recognize those fearful thoughts without automatically believing them became one of the most important parts of my emotional healing. Whenever I noticed my mind beginning to race, I would pause, take several slow breaths, and use self-hypnosis to imagine turning down the volume on fear. I wasn't ignoring my health or pretending everything was fine. I was simply quieting unnecessary alarm bells so I could think more clearly and respond with calm instead of panic.

Scan Anxiety—When Waiting Feels Like the Hardest Part

If you've ever felt anxious before a scan, mammogram, blood test, or follow-up appointment, please know you are far from alone. Cancer survivors have even given it a name—**scanxiety**. Sometimes, I found that the waiting was harder than the appointment itself. Days before a scheduled test, my imagination could create countless "what if" scenarios that had no basis in fact, yet they still felt very real. Many survivors describe difficulty sleeping before an appointment, feeling distracted at work, becoming irritable with loved ones, or thinking about little else. I certainly had those moments.

I also discovered that I wasn't the only one. While attending physical therapy to strengthen my core, I met a woman I'll call **Dana**. (Not her real name.) Knowing that I was a hypnotherapist, she shared that she had been treated for ovarian cancer about a year earlier. Recently, she had begun experiencing some discomfort, and although it could have been caused by any number of things, her oncologist wanted to order a follow-up scan to rule out a recurrence. As she waited for the results, her anxiety grew. She admitted she wasn't sleeping well, her mind constantly replayed worst-case scenarios, and she found it difficult to think about anything else.

I offered to guide Dana through hypnosis to help her manage the waiting. Rather than focusing on what might happen, I encouraged her mind to remain grounded in the present moment. I suggested that with each slow, comfortable breath she could release more tension and become increasingly calm. I reminded her that her mind did not have to solve a problem that had not yet been identified. Together, we replaced frightening "what if" thoughts with reassuring reminders such as, *"Right now, I am safe. Right now, I am simply waiting for information."* I also suggested that each night she could drift into a deep, peaceful sleep, allowing her body to rest and restore itself while her unconscious mind quietly held on to feelings of confidence, hope, and inner calm.

A few days later, Dana happily shared her news. Her scan was completely clear. Although her doctors still needed to determine the cause of her discomfort, it was **not** a recurrence of her cancer. Seeing the relief on her face reminded me once again how powerful our thoughts can be while we wait—and how important it is not to let fear write a story before we know the facts.

Dana's experience reinforced something I had been learning on my own. Waiting for medical results is never easy, but worrying cannot change those results. It can only rob us of today's peace.

Self-hypnosis became one of my most valuable tools before my own medical appointments. Before leaving for a scan or follow-up visit, I would spend a few quiet minutes relaxing my body and slowing my breathing. I imagined myself walking confidently into my doctor's office, feeling calm, comfortable, and in control. I pictured myself greeting the staff with a smile, listening carefully as my oncologist explained my results, and responding with confidence no matter what was discussed. I often imagined a control room in my mind where I could gently turn down the dial labeled **Fear** and turn up the dials marked **Calm**, **Trust**, **Hope**, and **Strength**. I reminded myself that I could not control the results of the scan, but I could control how I experienced the waiting. By rehearsing calm instead of catastrophe, I found that my body relaxed, my sleep improved, and I was able to walk into each appointment with greater peace and confidence.

I eventually realized that waiting is part of every cancer journey. Suffering through the waiting doesn't have to be.

Every Ache Is Not Cancer

One of the hardest lessons I had to learn was that not every ache, pain, or unusual sensation meant my cancer had returned. Before cancer, a headache was simply a headache. After cancer, my mind could quickly turn it into something much more frightening. The same was true for sore muscles, fatigue, or an unexpected pain. I had to remind myself that life still happens. People pull muscles, catch colds, sleep in awkward positions, and simply grow older. Cancer had changed the way I interpreted normal sensations. Once I recognized that, I was able to respond differently. Instead of immediately assuming the worst, I learned to become curious rather than fearful. If something truly concerned me, I contacted my healthcare provider. If it didn't, I gently reminded myself that my body was still healing and that not every physical sensation deserved a catastrophic explanation.

During self-hypnosis, I often imagined pressing a pause button whenever fear tried to race ahead of the facts. That simple mental image reminded me to breathe, slow down, and ask myself, "What evidence do I actually have right now?" More often than not, that brief pause was enough to quiet my anxious thoughts.

Waiting Can Be Harder Than Treatment

This may sound surprising, but I've heard many cancer survivors say that life after treatment was, in some ways, more difficult than treatment itself. During treatment, every day had structure. There were appointments, medications, tests, and healthcare professionals checking on me. My job was simple: show up, follow the treatment plan, and keep moving forward one day at a time. Then treatment ended. Everyone celebrated because I was "finished," but emotionally I was just beginning another phase of my journey. Friends expected life to return to normal, yet inside I was still learning how to trust my body again. Healing didn't happen the day my last treatment ended. It unfolded gradually, one ordinary day at a time. I had to learn patience with myself and trust that emotional healing follows its own timetable.

During self-hypnosis, I often pictured myself walking through a beautiful garden. Every flower bloomed in its own season. None were rushed, and none were behind schedule. That gentle image reminded me that my own healing would also unfold exactly as it was meant to.

Fear of Recurrence

Perhaps the greatest fear many cancer survivors carry is the fear that cancer will return. For some people, that fear gradually fades over time. For others, it quietly returns before every follow-up appointment or unexpectedly appears after hearing about someone else's diagnosis. There is no right or wrong way to experience these feelings. What matters is learning that fear does not have to make your decisions for you. I came to realize that I might never completely eliminate fear, and surprisingly, that realization brought me peace. The goal was never to become fearless. The goal was to become stronger than my fear. I began reminding myself, "I will deal with today, today. If tomorrow brings a challenge, I will meet it tomorrow." Those simple words helped bring my attention back to the present.

During self-hypnosis, I often imagined myself driving down a peaceful road with fear sitting quietly in the passenger seat. Fear could ride along from time to time, but it no longer held the steering wheel. I did.

Living Between Checkups

Life after cancer can sometimes feel as though it is measured from one follow-up appointment to the next. You have a scan or checkup, receive reassuring news, breathe a sigh of relief, and begin living normally again. Then, as the next appointment approaches, the anxiety slowly returns. At one point I realized that I didn't want to spend months waiting to live until after my next doctor's visit. Life was happening right now. There were sunsets to enjoy, vacations to take, books to read, friends to visit, family to hug, music to enjoy, and laughter to share. Cancer had already taken enough from me. I wasn't willing to let fear take today as well.

Self-hypnosis helped anchor me in the present moment. I would imagine today's date written clearly before me and remind myself that this was the only day I was actually living. Tomorrow would come soon enough. Today deserved my full attention.

When Thoughts Begin to Spiral

Our minds are remarkably creative, and unfortunately, anxiety often directs that creativity toward imagining worst-case scenarios. One fearful thought can quickly become ten, and before we know it, we've created an entire future that exists only in our imagination. One of the most valuable lessons I learned was that there is a tremendous difference between saying, "My cancer is back," and saying, "I'm having the thought that my cancer is back." That small change in wording creates emotional breathing room. Thoughts are not facts. They are simply thoughts, and thoughts come and go.

During self-hypnosis, I often imagined each fearful thought resting on a leaf floating gently down a peaceful stream. I didn't have to fight the thought or pretend it wasn't there. I simply watched it drift away, allowing my attention to return to the present moment where I was safe.

Choosing Hope Without Denying Reality

Hope is sometimes misunderstood. It isn't pretending everything will always be fine, nor is it ignoring medical advice or denying difficult emotions. Real hope is much stronger than that. Hope says, "I don't know exactly what tomorrow will bring, but I know I can meet it." It allows us to make plans, celebrate birthdays, laugh with friends, enjoy vacations, and appreciate ordinary moments, even while living with uncertainty. Cancer taught me many lessons, but perhaps the greatest was this: life has always been uncertain. Cancer simply made me more aware of that truth. Once I accepted it, I found myself appreciating each ordinary day more deeply than ever before.

Self-hypnosis became a gentle reminder of that lesson. I would picture myself standing beneath a beautiful rainbow after a passing storm, feeling the warmth of the sun returning and remembering that storms do not last forever. With every slow breath, I allowed myself to absorb a little more hope, a little more strength, and a little more gratitude for the gift of today. That, perhaps, is one of the most beautiful rainbows we can discover after the storm.

Self-Hypnosis Suggestions for the "What Ifs"

- I choose to focus on what I know today rather than what I fear about tomorrow.
- I release the need to predict the future.
- I can handle today, one step at a time.
- My mind becomes calmer with every slow, comfortable breath.
- I replace fearful thoughts with hopeful possibilities.
- I am stronger than I sometimes realize.
- I trust my ability to cope with whatever comes my way.
- I do not have to solve tomorrow's problems today.
- I allow my body to relax and my mind to become quiet.
- I let go of thoughts that no longer serve me.
- I focus on what I can control and release what I cannot.
- I choose faith over fear.

- Hope grows stronger each day.
- My doctors and medical team are guiding me with skill and compassion.
- My body is responding to treatment in healthy and positive ways.
- Every day I become more confident and more resilient.
- My mind and body work together to support my healing.
- I deserve peace, comfort, and hope.
- I am safe in this present moment.
- Each day brings new reasons to be hopeful.
- I am more than my diagnosis.
- I choose courage over worry.
- I trust that I will find the strength I need when I need it.
- I look toward the future with hope instead of fear.
- I give myself permission to relax and enjoy today.
- My thoughts become peaceful, calm, and optimistic.
- I welcome feelings of confidence, gratitude, and inner peace.
- I am healing one day, one step, and one breath at a time.

Also see Appendix E

Whenever my mind asks, "What if something goes wrong?" I gently answer, "What if everything turns out better than I imagined?"

Chapter 12

Lifestyle and Habit Changes

Healthy Choices That Support Healing and Lifelong Wellness

A cancer diagnosis is not a judgment about how you've lived your life. Many people who eat well, exercise regularly, and take good care of themselves still develop cancer. Please don't blame yourself or spend time wondering, *"What did I do wrong?"* Instead, look at your diagnosis as an opportunity to become even more intentional about caring for yourself and creating habits that support healing, recovery, and long-term health.

After my diagnosis, I came to an important realization. While I couldn't change the fact that I had cancer, I could influence many of the choices I made each day. Cancer taught me that every healthy choice mattered—not because it guaranteed the cancer would never return, but because each choice made me stronger, healthier, and better able to enjoy life.

Recovery isn't only about completing surgery, chemotherapy, or radiation. It's also about rebuilding your body, your mind, and your spirit—one healthy habit at a time. The encouraging news is that you don't have to change everything overnight. Lasting change usually happens through small, consistent steps.

About six months after my breast cancer surgery, Heidi, a staff member at New York-Presbyterian Hospital, approached me about participating in a ten-year research study. The study was based on the premise that women who lost at least 10 percent of their body weight after a breast cancer diagnosis might significantly reduce their risk of recurrence. At the time, I weighed 180 pounds, and I gladly agreed to participate.

That decision became the beginning of my own wellness journey. As I learned more about nutrition, exercise, behavior change, and the power of hypnosis to create lasting habits, I lost the weight—but I gained something even more valuable: a healthier lifestyle. The experience eventually inspired me to write *Weighing in on Hypnosis: Lifestyle and Habit Changes for Weight Loss Success.* If you would like more detailed information about topics such as healthy eating, exercise, sleep, stress management, and creating lasting lifestyle habits, you may find it to be a helpful companion to this book.

Because self-hypnosis became such an important part of my own healing journey, I wrote *Self-Hypnosis: Easy as 1, 2, 3: 3 Minutes to Change Your Life.* Throughout this book, you'll find simple self-hypnosis suggestions that complement each chapter. If you would like to learn the process in greater depth and develop a regular self-hypnosis practice, that book provides additional instruction and guided exercises.

Some of the lifestyle changes I made included losing weight, eating more fruits and vegetables, limiting processed foods, drinking more water, and incorporating regular movement—

mostly walking, which felt both manageable and restorative. Self-care also became a priority. I improved my sleep habits, paid more attention to grooming, and treated myself to a monthly massage, which I quickly discovered was not a luxury but part of my healing. I practiced self-hypnosis regularly to calm my mind and support my body's natural healing response. I became more intentional about managing stress, keeping my follow-up appointments, staying socially connected, protecting my emotional well-being, and making time for the people and activities that brought me joy.

The lifestyle changes that follow are not meant to be another checklist or set of rules. Think of them as possibilities—small, positive steps that can help you regain a sense of control and support your health and well-being. You don't have to make every change at once. Choose one place to begin, build on your success, and remember that every healthy choice is an investment in your future.

Here are some of the lifestyle habits that helped me move from simply surviving cancer to truly thriving after it.

1. Nourish Your Body

Your body has been through an incredible journey. Surgery, chemotherapy, radiation, and medications all place extra demands on your physical health. Eating a balanced diet rich in fruits, vegetables, whole grains, lean proteins, and healthy fats provides the nutrients your body needs to heal, rebuild, and regain strength. Rather than striving for a perfect diet, focus on making healthy choices more often than not. Every nourishing meal is an investment in your recovery.

2. Stay Hydrated

Water plays an essential role in nearly every function of your body. Staying well hydrated helps transport nutrients, regulate body temperature, support healthy digestion, lubricate joints, and maintain healthy kidney function. During and after cancer treatment, proper hydration may also help reduce fatigue, ease constipation, improve concentration, and promote your body's natural healing processes. Carry a reusable water bottle with you, sip water throughout the day, and choose water more often than sugary beverages. If plain water isn't appealing, try adding slices of lemon, cucumber, berries, or fresh mint for a refreshing change. Every glass of water is another simple way to support your health and well-being.

3. Maintain a Healthy Weight

Cancer treatment can affect your weight in different ways. Some people lose weight because of treatment side effects, while others gain weight due to medications, fatigue, or reduced activity. The goal is not achieving an ideal number on the scale but maintaining a healthy weight that supports your overall well-being. Even small, sustainable changes in eating habits and physical activity can improve your energy level, reduce your risk of other chronic illnesses, and help you feel your best.

4. Move Your Body

Physical activity is one of the most beneficial things you can do after a cancer diagnosis. Exercise can help reduce fatigue, improve mood, strengthen muscles, maintain bone health, and increase your overall quality of life. You don't have to run marathons or spend hours in a gym. A daily walk, gentle stretching, dancing, gardening, or swimming can all make a meaningful difference. Start where you are and gradually increase your activity as your body allows.

5. Prioritize Sleep

Quality sleep is essential for healing. During treatment and recovery, many people struggle with insomnia, interrupted sleep, or fatigue. Establishing a regular bedtime routine, limiting screen time before bed, creating a peaceful sleep environment, and practicing relaxation or self-hypnosis can all promote better rest. Even if sleep doesn't come easily every night, making it a priority helps your body and mind recover.

6. Manage Stress

A cancer diagnosis naturally brings uncertainty, fear, and emotional ups and downs. While stress does not cause cancer, learning healthy ways to manage it can improve both emotional and physical well-being. Deep breathing, meditation, prayer, journaling, spending time in nature, talking with supportive friends, and practicing self-hypnosis are all effective ways to reduce stress and restore a sense of calm. Caring for your emotional health is just as important as caring for your physical health.

7. If You Smoke, Make Quitting a Priority

If you smoke, quitting is one of the most important steps you can take to improve your health. Stopping smoking can enhance healing, improve lung and heart function, reduce the risk of treatment complications, and lower the risk of developing additional cancers. Quitting is not easy, but many effective resources, medications, counseling programs, and hypnosis techniques are available to help you succeed. Every day without smoking is a victory worth celebrating.

8. Limit Alcohol

Research continues to show that alcohol consumption is linked to an increased risk of several types of cancer. If you choose to drink, consider reducing the amount or avoiding alcohol altogether. Many people discover that replacing alcoholic beverages with flavored sparkling water, herbal tea, or other healthy alternatives becomes easier than they expected. Small adjustments can support your long-term health without feeling like a sacrifice.

9. Keep Your Follow-Up Appointments

Completing treatment does not mean your medical care is over. Regular follow-up visits allow your healthcare team to monitor your recovery, detect any changes early, manage side effects, and answer your questions. Be sure to attend scheduled appointments, complete recommended screenings, and take medications exactly as prescribed. These visits provide reassurance and help ensure you continue receiving the best possible care.

10. Care for Your Emotional Health

Healing involves much more than your physical body. Many survivors experience fear of recurrence, anxiety, sadness, or unexpected emotional challenges long after treatment has ended. Seeking support is a sign of strength, not weakness. Whether through counseling, support groups, trusted friends, family members, or spiritual communities, sharing your thoughts and feelings can lighten the emotional burden and remind you that you do not have to face this journey alone.

11. Build Healthy Relationships

Cancer often reveals who will stand beside you during life's most difficult moments. It may strengthen some relationships while changing others. Surround yourself with people who encourage, support, and uplift you. Accept offers of help when they are given, communicate your needs honestly, and don't be afraid to establish healthy boundaries with those who increase your stress. Meaningful relationships are a powerful source of comfort and resilience.

12. Make Time for Joy

Perhaps one of the greatest lessons cancer teaches is that life should not be put on hold while waiting for perfect health or perfect circumstances. Make time for the activities that bring you happiness, whether it's spending time with loved ones, taking a walk, reading a good book, dancing, traveling, creating art, working on a puzzle, singing karaoke, or simply watching a beautiful sunset. Moments of joy are not distractions from healing—they are an important part of it. Every smile, every laugh, and every cherished memory remind us that we are living life, not simply surviving it.

13. Practice Self-Hypnosis

Throughout this book, you will find self-hypnosis suggestions woven into many chapters, designed to support you wherever you are in your journey. These techniques can help you relax your body, calm your mind, improve sleep, ease anxiety, and strengthen your ability to cope with treatment and recovery. Self-hypnosis is not about "losing control," but rather about gently guiding your mind toward a more peaceful and supportive state. The more you practice, the more natural it becomes to shift into this calm, focused awareness whenever you need it. Think of these moments as a daily reset—small pockets of time where you can step back from fear or stress and reconnect with your inner strength, resilience, and healing resources.

14. Self-Care Isn't Selfish

One lesson cancer taught me is that taking care of yourself isn't selfish—it's necessary.

Before my diagnosis, like so many people, I often put everyone else's needs ahead of my own. There was always another phone call to make, another errand to run, another project to finish. After cancer, I began to realize that if I wanted to be there for the people I loved, I first had to take care of myself.

Self-care doesn't have to be expensive or time-consuming. Often, it's the simple things that restore both body and spirit.

Some of the self-care practices that helped me include:

- Practicing self-hypnosis and relaxation every day.
- Taking walks whenever I felt up to it.
- Eating nourishing foods that supported my recovery.
- Getting enough sleep and allowing myself to rest without guilt.
- Spending time with Robert, family, and friends.
- Reading books that inspired and encouraged me.
- Listening to music that lifted my spirits.
- Ballroom dancing again when I was able.
- Traveling and creating new memories.
- Spending quiet time with Nutmeg curled up beside me.
- Practicing gratitude by noticing something good in every day.

One unexpected blessing has been the opportunity to share stories with participants in the Adelphi University New York

Statewide Breast Cancer Support Program's semiannual Art Therapy Zoom programs. Each time I meet with these remarkable survivors, I leave inspired by their courage, creativity, and willingness to support one another. Watching them express themselves through art while learning new ways to reduce stress reminds me that healing comes in many forms. It doesn't happen only through surgery, chemotherapy, or radiation. It also happens through connection, creativity, laughter, hope, and caring for ourselves emotionally as well as physically.

You cannot always choose what life brings you, but after a cancer diagnosis, you can choose how you respond. While you may not have control over everything that happens, you do have control over many of the choices you make each day. Every healthy habit you develop, every act of self-care, and every positive change you make is an investment in your health, your well-being, and your future. These choices may seem small on their own, but over time they can have a profound impact on how you feel, how you heal, and how you live. They are a reminder that you are not powerless. You have the ability to influence both your mind and your body in ways that can help you not only survive cancer, but truly thrive beyond it.

As I embraced these lifestyle changes, I discovered that healing involved much more than caring for my body. The greatest challenge wasn't always physical—it was learning to live with uncertainty. Fear of recurrence, waiting for test results, and wondering what the future might hold became part of my journey. Learning how to quiet those fears and find peace in the midst of uncertainty became just as important as any healthy habit I adopted—and that is where our journey takes us next.

Cancer changed my priorities. It taught me that taking time to care for myself allows me to better care for others. I hope you'll give yourself that same gift. You deserve it.

Fortunately, I discovered that many of the same tools that helped me care for my body—especially self-hypnosis—also became some of my greatest allies in calming my mind. In the next chapter, we'll explore how to accept help.

Self-Hypnosis Suggestions

Creating Healthy Lifestyle Habits

- Every healthy choice I make supports my healing.
- I enjoy taking good care of my body because it deserves kindness and respect.
- Each day, healthy habits become easier and more natural.
- I choose foods that nourish my body and give me energy.
- I eat slowly, comfortably, and mindfully.
- I recognize when I am comfortably satisfied and stop eating with ease.
- Drinking water throughout the day has become a healthy habit that I enjoy.
- I look forward to moving my body in ways that feel good to me.
- Every step I take strengthens my body and lifts my spirits.
- Exercise becomes easier because I focus on how good I feel afterward.
- I listen to my body's signals and give it the rest it needs.
- I make sleep a priority because restful sleep supports healing.
- Each day I become more organized in taking my medications and following my treatment plan.

- I enjoy finding healthy ways to manage stress.
- Deep breathing helps me feel calm, relaxed, and in control.
- I let go of habits that no longer serve me.
- I replace unhealthy habits with healthier ones, one step at a time.
- I celebrate every success, no matter how small.
- I am patient with myself as I make lasting lifestyle changes.
- I choose progress, not perfection.
- Every healthy decision I make today benefits my future.
- My body appreciates the loving care I give it each day.
- I am becoming healthier, stronger, and more confident every day.
- I believe in my ability to create lasting, positive habits.
- I am committed to living a healthy, meaningful, and joyful life.

Closing Suggestions

- Every day, I find it easier to make choices that support my health and well-being.
- My healthy habits are becoming automatic.
- I feel proud of the positive changes I am making.
- I am creating a lifestyle that supports healing, hope, and lifelong wellness.
- One healthy choice at a time, I am building a brighter future.
- Every healthy choice I make is a gift of love to myself and an investment in my future.

Chapter 13

The Gift of Accepting Help

A Mitzvah: A Blessing for Both the Giver and the Receiver

Although my breast cancer journey changed my life in profound ways, it wasn't my first experience with cancer.

In 2008, I was diagnosed with kidney cancer. Fortunately, it was discovered early, and I underwent a partial nephrectomy. Because the tumor was completely removed during surgery, I did not require chemotherapy or radiation.

At the time, my late husband, Tony, had broken his leg and was recovering in a rehabilitation facility. My original surgeon explained that he could perform the surgery using the traditional approach, but my recovery would likely take about six weeks. Knowing that Tony would soon be returning home and would need my help, he selflessly referred me to a colleague who specialized in robotic surgery. The robotic procedure reduced my recovery time to approximately three weeks. I will always be grateful to that surgeon for putting my needs ahead of his own by referring me to someone who could help me recover more quickly.

The timing could not have worked out better. Tony was expected to remain in rehabilitation for another four weeks, giving me enough time to recover before he came home. I was able to care for myself, but I soon realized that recovering from surgery is much easier when you allow others to help.

One dear friend, whose husband had recently been laid off from work, brought me a home-cooked dinner every few days. Knowing the financial challenges they were facing made her generosity even more meaningful. I gratefully accepted her kindness. Another friend offered to do my grocery shopping whenever I needed anything, and I happily accepted her help as well.

At first, accepting help didn't come naturally. Like many people, I was accustomed to being the one helping others. Learning to receive was just as important as learning to give.

At the time, I had no idea that this experience was quietly preparing me for another cancer journey years later—one that would test me in ways I could never have imagined, but would also teach me some of life's greatest lessons. Years later, when I was diagnosed with breast cancer, I came to understand the value of allowing others to walk beside me, and my husband, Robert, became my caregiver, standing by me through surgery, chemotherapy, radiation, and the challenges of recovery.

If family members, friends, neighbors, or members of your community offer to help, accept their kindness with gratitude. And if you need help, don't be afraid to ask. People often want to do something meaningful when someone they care about is facing cancer, but they don't always know what to do. If someone asks, "What can I do to help?" tell them exactly what you need. It might be preparing a meal, picking up groceries, driving you to an appointment, walking the dog, or simply sitting quietly with you. Most people genuinely want to help—they just need to know how.

There is a beautiful concept in the Jewish tradition called a *mitzvah*. While the word is often translated as "a good deed," it is much more than that. A mitzvah is an act of kindness, compassion, or generosity that becomes a blessing to both the person who receives it and the person who gives it.

For a long time, I thought accepting help meant I was imposing on others. Eventually, I realized just the opposite was true. By allowing someone to bring a meal, drive me to an appointment, shop for groceries, or simply spend time with me, I was giving them the opportunity to perform their own *mitzvah*—an act of kindness and compassion. When someone reaches out with a sincere offer to help, graciously accept it. You are not taking something away from them—you are giving them the opportunity to make a meaningful difference in your life. Sometimes the greatest gift we receive is allowing someone else the joy of giving. What begins as an act of kindness becomes a blessing for both of you.

Looking back on both cancer journeys, I can clearly see that each one taught me the same lesson: cancer is not a journey anyone should travel alone.

Sometimes the greatest gift we receive is allowing someone else the joy of giving.

Chapter 14

Caring for the Caregiver

Supporting Those who Support Us

When someone you love is facing cancer, illness, or recovery, it is easy to put all of your attention on them and very little on yourself. Caregivers often become the quiet heroes in the background — driving to appointments, organizing medications, preparing meals, listening to fears, managing insurance forms, and trying to keep daily life moving forward. Many do this while still working, caring for children, or managing households of their own.

Caregiving comes from love. But even love can become exhausting when there is little rest, little support, and no time to breathe.

When his wife's breast cancer metastasized to her brain, Brian arranged to work from home so he could be near her and help care for her. (See Joanne's story: A Different Kind of Healing - Chapter 15.) At the time, he was managing warehouse operations on-site, overseeing the daily activities of a distribution center to ensure products were received, stored, picked, packed, and shipped efficiently and accurately.

As his wife's needs increased, Brian transitioned into a warehouse logistics manager role. Instead of focusing on the warehouse floor and supervising daily physical operations, his work became more systems- and data-focused. From home, he was able to manage the flow of operations digitally through reports, dashboards, phone calls, remote coordination, and warehouse management systems, allowing him to continue working while also being present for his wife.

In addition to his job, Brian found himself taking over most of the daily household responsibilities, including cooking, cleaning, shopping, laundry, and other chores. They had two college-age children who helped when they were home, but most of the responsibility fell on Brian's shoulders.

Like many caregivers, Brian wanted to do everything himself.

Whenever neighbors or friends asked what they could do to help, his usual response was, "Thanks, I've got this."

But as the weeks passed, the physical and emotional demands of caring for Joanne began to take their toll. I offered to work with Brian privately and teach him self-hypnosis to help him relax, recharge, and better manage the stress of caregiving. Although he appreciated the offer, he never took me up on it.

Even so, I encouraged him to do something that many caregivers find surprisingly difficult—accept help when it is offered.

Instead of saying, "I'm fine," I suggested he be specific about what he needed. Little by little, he did just that.

He gave one neighbor a grocery shopping list. Another neighbor, who was a wonderful cook, prepared meals he could simply heat and serve. He even asked a close friend to spend an evening with Joanne so he could go to a local pub, unwind for a few hours, and enjoy some much-needed time with friends.

No one can pour from an empty cup. Caregivers need moments to rest and restore themselves, too. By allowing others to help, Brian was not letting Joanne down—he was giving himself the strength to continue caring for her with the love and compassion she needed.

The bottom line is this: when people ask how they can help, be specific about what you need. Most people truly want to help, but they often do not know what would be useful.

And just as importantly, remember to take care of your own physical and emotional needs. Make sure you get enough sleep, exercise regularly, and eat nutritious foods. If you do not take care of yourself first, it becomes much harder to care for another.

Many caregivers tell themselves they have to be strong every moment of every day. But caregiving is not about doing everything alone. Sometimes strength means allowing others to help carry the load.

Many caregivers tell themselves:

- "I have to stay strong."
- "I shouldn't complain."
- "They are the one with cancer, not me."
- "I'll take care of myself later."

But later has a way of never arriving.

The truth is this: caregivers need care too.

You cannot continually pour from an empty cup. Physical exhaustion, emotional overload, poor sleep, irritability, forgetfulness, anxiety, sadness, and even resentment can quietly build when self-care is ignored for too long. None of this means you are weak or selfish. It means you are human.

Taking care of yourself is not abandoning the person you love. It is strengthening yourself so you can continue showing up with compassion, patience, and steadiness.

Sometimes self-care is something small:

- Sitting quietly with a cup of tea before the house wakes up
- Taking a short walk outside
- Listening to music
- Saying "yes" when someone offers help
- Allowing yourself to cry
- Taking an uninterrupted nap
- Laughing without guilt
- Going to lunch with a friend
- Taking ten slow breaths in the car before entering another appointment

Small moments matter.

Caregivers often live in a constant state of vigilance, always waiting for the next phone call, test result, symptom, or emergency. The nervous system rarely gets a chance to settle. Hypnosis and relaxation techniques can help calm the body and mind, reduce stress, improve sleep, and restore emotional balance.

Self-Care Hypnotic Suggestions for Caregivers

As you relax, allow these thoughts to settle gently into your mind:

- Every breath helps me release tension I no longer need to carry.
- I am allowed to rest.
- Taking care of myself helps me care for others more effectively.
- I do not have to carry everything alone.
- It is safe to ask for help.
- I release guilt about taking time for myself.
- My body deserves nourishment, rest, and care.
- Calmness can return to me one breath at a time.
- I can handle today without having to solve everything about tomorrow.
- Peace is still possible, even during difficult times.
- I give myself permission to pause.
- My mind and body know how to recover from stress.
- I deserve moments of comfort and joy.
- I am doing the best I can.
- I am stronger than I realize, and gentler with myself each day.

Brief Caregiver Relaxation Exercise

Find a comfortable position and allow your eyes to close.

Take a slow deep breath in… and gently exhale.

Again… breathing in calm… and breathing out tension.

Imagine a soft wave of relaxation beginning at the top of your head and slowly moving downward through your body… relaxing your forehead… your jaw… your shoulders… your arms… your chest… your stomach… your legs… and your feet.

For the next few moments, there is nowhere you need to be and nothing you need to solve.

Imagine placing every worry, responsibility, and fear into a basket beside you. You are not throwing them away. You are simply setting them down for a little while.

Allow your mind to rest.

Imagine yourself in a peaceful place — perhaps sitting quietly near the ocean, resting in a garden, sitting on a porch in the early morning light, or walking slowly through the woods. Notice the calmness there. Notice the quiet.

And as you rest in this peaceful place, remind yourself:

I matter too.

My wellbeing is important.

Rest is not weakness.

Taking care of myself is part of the healing process too.

Allow that feeling of calm to settle deeply into your mind and body, knowing you can return to this peaceful feeling whenever you need it.

Chapter 15

A Different Kind of Healing

Joanne's Story

The story you are about to read is different from the others in this book.

Joanne was a hypnosis client who graciously gave me permission, while she was still alive, to share her journey in the hope that it might help others facing a similar path. I have thought about her often as I wrote this book, and I am honored to tell her story. In many ways, working with Joanne inspired me to write this book. Her courage, honesty, and determination reminded me that even when a cure is no longer possible, there is still so much we can do to ease suffering, restore hope, and improve the quality of life.

Not every cancer story ends the way we hope. While many people survive and thrive after treatment, some receive the heartbreaking news that their cancer has returned or spread. Joanne was one of those people. Although hypnosis could not change her diagnosis, it helped change how she experienced the months that followed. It gave her greater peace, helped her manage many of her symptoms, and allowed her to focus on what mattered most—the people she loved and the time she had with them.

Joanne lived in London, England, and found me through my website. She had originally been diagnosed with breast cancer in 2013. Ten years later, in 2023, she learned that the cancer had metastasized to her brain and that she now had Stage IV cancer. Her oncologist estimated that she might have about a year to live.

She contacted me because she wanted help managing the emotional and physical challenges she was facing. Over the next four months, we met for nine hypnosis sessions over Zoom. Together we worked on reducing stress and anxiety, managing chemotherapy side effects, increasing comfort, improving sleep, and helping her feel more in control during an uncertain time.

Before retiring because of her illness, Joanne had been a language teacher, teaching French, German, and Spanish. She loved her work and enjoyed helping others learn. One of the greatest emotional burdens she carried was guilt. Several years earlier, her oncologist had prescribed hormone-blocking medication and recommended that she take it for ten years. After seven years, she stopped taking the medication because of the side effects. About a year later, the cancer returned.

Like many people facing a recurrence, Joanne questioned whether she had made the wrong decision. She wondered if stopping the medication had somehow caused the cancer to come back. While continuing prescribed treatment can reduce the risk of recurrence, no one can know with certainty why an individual's cancer returns. Rather than dwelling on "what if," our work focused on helping Joanne release her self-blame, practice self-compassion, and devote her emotional energy to making the most of each day.

During our first session, I asked Joanne three questions that I often ask my hypnosis clients:

What do you want?

How do you want to feel?

How will you know when you've achieved it?

Her answers have stayed with me ever since.

"I want to feel in control of my body."

"I want to feel that I have accomplished something with my life."

"I want to be able to say goodbye to my family without regret."

Those simple yet profound answers became the foundation for everything we worked on together.

Joanne had been married to her husband, Andrew, for twenty-five years. When her illness progressed, Andrew arranged to transition from working in an office to working from home so he could be with her and help care for her. They had two children—a twenty-year-old son and an eighteen-year-old daughter—who were both away at college but came home on weekends whenever they could. Joanne spoke often about how grateful she was for the love and support of her family.

Over the course of our nine sessions together, I taught Joanne how to enter hypnosis using the Progressive Relaxation Technique and how to use the Control Room Technique to manage pain and discomfort (both techniques are described in the Appendix). With practice, she became increasingly comfortable using these skills on her own between our sessions.

At the beginning of each appointment, we reviewed the previous week. I asked what had gone well, what challenges she had encountered, which hypnosis suggestions had been most helpful, and whether she had been practicing the techniques we had discussed. Those conversations allowed us to build on her successes and tailor each session to her current needs.

Because Andrew was Joanne's primary caregiver, I also offered to meet with him separately. Caregivers often devote so much of themselves to caring for someone they love that they neglect their own emotional and physical well-being. Supporting the caregiver is an important part of supporting the patient.

Our first session centered on helping Joanne release the guilt she felt about stopping her hormone-blocking medication before the recommended ten years. Through hypnosis, we focused on replacing self-blame with self-compassion and accepting that she had made the best decision she could with the information and circumstances she had at the time.

During our second session, Joanne told me that one of her greatest frustrations was difficulty sleeping. Like many people facing cancer, she found that when she went to bed at night, her mind became filled with worries and "what if" thoughts. We focused on helping her quiet those thoughts, relax both her mind and body, and allow sleep to come naturally. I taught Joanne self-hypnosis techniques specifically for sleep and created suggestions to help her fall asleep more easily, remain asleep throughout the night, and gently return to sleep if she awakened during the night. Because I wanted her to have additional resources, I also recommended a wonderful book written by my colleague, Robert Martel, *I Am Sleeping Now.* Joanne purchased the book and faithfully practiced several of the self-hypnosis exercises it contained, adding them to the techniques we were working on together.

Each hypnosis session focused on one specific concern, and occasionally we devoted two sessions to the same issue when it needed additional attention. Rather than giving Joanne generic stress-reduction suggestions, I created suggestions that reflected the real challenges she was facing each day. We worked on letting go of the guilt she felt about not helping Andrew more around the house, giving herself permission to rest without feeling selfish, finishing the jumpers she was knitting (she smiled as she explained that in England, a "jumper" is what we call a sweater in the United States), and gradually rebuilding her strength by taking short daily walks. I have found that people respond most deeply when hypnosis speaks directly to the circumstances of their own lives rather than using only general suggestions.

One of those bright spots was a planned trip to Cambridge with Andrew. Rather than allowing cancer to become the center of every conversation, we spent time talking about the pleasures that still awaited her. Maintaining hope doesn't mean pretending cancer isn't there. It means continuing to find reasons to live fully, appreciate each day, and create meaningful moments with the people you love.

About six months after our final session together, I received an email from Andrew. He wanted to let me know how much our work together had meant to Joanne and to thank me for helping make her final months a little easier and more peaceful.

He ended his email with words that touched my heart. Joanne had passed away peacefully in her sleep, surrounded by himself and their two children.

Although Joanne's cancer could not be cured, I truly believe hypnosis helped improve the quality of the time she had left. It eased her anxiety, helped her manage pain and sleep more comfortably, softened the burden of guilt she carried, and allowed her to focus on what mattered most—loving her family and living each day as fully as possible.

Joanne's story reminds us that healing does not always mean curing. Sometimes healing means finding comfort, peace, acceptance, and hope, even in life's most difficult moments. I will always be grateful that she trusted me to be part of her journey and gave me permission to share her story so that it might bring comfort and encouragement to others.

Hypnotic Suggestions for Releasing Guilt and Self-Blame

- You release the burden of self-blame, knowing that you made the best decisions you could with the information and circumstances you had at the time.
- You recognize that many factors influence cancer, and you no longer carry the weight of believing you caused your illness to return.
- You forgive yourself with the same kindness and compassion you would offer a dear friend facing the same circumstances.
- Each day, you choose to spend your emotional energy on healing, hope, and the people you love rather than on regrets about the past.

- You accept that the past cannot be changed, but each new day offers opportunities to find meaning, love, and moments of joy.
- You allow feelings of peace to replace feelings of guilt, knowing that self-compassion supports your emotional well-being.
- You are more than your diagnosis. You are a loving wife, mother, friend, and a person whose life continues to have purpose and value.
- You let go of "what if" thoughts and gently bring your attention back to the present moment, where you can make the greatest difference.
- Every day, you become more accepting of yourself, your journey, and your remarkable strength in facing life's challenges.
- You move forward with courage, hope, and self-kindness, knowing that you deserve peace as much as anyone else.

Hypnotic Suggestions for Restful Sleep

- Each evening, when your head touches the pillow, your mind and body recognize that it is time to rest.
- Your breathing becomes slow, steady, and comfortable, and with every breath you relax more deeply.
- You do not have to make sleep happen. As you relax, sleep comes naturally and effortlessly.
- Any thoughts that enter your mind simply drift away like clouds floating across a peaceful sky, leaving your mind calm and quiet.
- You fall asleep more quickly each night, feeling safe, comfortable, and completely at ease.
- Throughout the night, your sleep is deep, peaceful, and restorative as your body renews and heals itself.

- If you awaken during the night, you remain calm, take a slow, relaxing breath, and easily drift back into a deep, comfortable sleep.
- Each morning you awaken feeling refreshed, energized, and ready to enjoy the day ahead.
- Every night your sleep becomes deeper, longer, and more refreshing than the night before.
- Healthy, restful sleep is becoming your new natural pattern, allowing your mind and body to function at their very best.

The following Self-Hypnosis suggestion can be very helpful if you wake during the night or feel anxious about not sleeping. It gives you a simple tool you can use independently to return to a relaxed state.

Whenever you place your hand over your heart and take three slow, comfortable breaths, your body immediately remembers this peaceful state of relaxation. The relaxation spreads through your entire body, signaling to your mind that it is safe to rest, safe to let go, and safe to sleep.

Stress and Anxiety

These suggestions fit Joanne's situation well because they reinforce **acceptance, purpose, contribution, and gentle activity** rather than focusing on what cancer has temporarily taken away. They also encourage her to celebrate small accomplishments and recognize that healing itself is productive.

Hypnotic Suggestions for Managing Stress and Anxiety

- Each day, you focus on what you are able to do rather than on what you cannot do today. Every small accomplishment is a meaningful step forward.

- As your body heals, you discover joy in simple pleasures—knitting another few rows, baking bread with your husband, helping prepare lunch, or sharing a quiet moment together.
- You release any unnecessary guilt about needing time to rest. Rest is not a sign of weakness; it is an important part of your healing.
- You trust that your family knows how deeply you love them, and each loving word, smile, or shared activity is a gift that means more than any household chore.
- You enjoy working a little at a time on the sweaters for your daughter and niece, knowing that every stitch is woven with love and brings you closer to completing this special gift.
- Each morning, you look forward to taking a short walk, even if it is only a few minutes. Every step strengthens your body, lifts your spirits, and supports your recovery.
- Your energy gradually increases each day. You naturally notice yourself doing a little more when your body is ready, always respecting your need for balance between activity and rest.
- You choose peaceful, encouraging thoughts. Whenever worry about the future appears, you gently return your attention to this moment, where you can heal, smile, and enjoy today.
- You appreciate every act of kindness your husband offers, and you allow yourself to receive his love and support with gratitude, knowing that accepting help today allows you to give again tomorrow.
- With every passing day, you become more confident in your body's remarkable ability to heal. You move forward with hope, patience, and the quiet certainty that brighter days lie ahead.

Chemotherapy affects people differently depending on the type of cancer, the specific drugs used, and the individual. Joanne experienced all of the typical side effects below in varying degrees, described in my Chemotherapy chapter.

Ten Hypnotic Suggestions for Coping with Chemotherapy

- Your body accepts each chemotherapy treatment as an important part of your healing. Every treatment is working with your body to help restore your health.
- You remain calm and comfortable before, during, and after each treatment. With every slow, relaxing breath, your body becomes more peaceful and at ease.
- If feelings of nausea begin, your stomach remains calm and settled. You feel increasingly comfortable, and your body knows how to find balance again.
- Each day your energy gradually returns. You naturally balance activity with rest, allowing your body to heal at its own comfortable pace.
- You sleep deeply and peacefully each night, giving your body the opportunity to restore, repair, and strengthen itself.
- Your mind remains clear and focused. You easily remember the things that are important to you, and your concentration improves a little more each day.
- You nourish your body with the foods and fluids that support healing. Your appetite naturally returns as your body is ready.
- You release fear and worry with every exhale. In their place, you welcome hope, confidence, and trust in your body's remarkable ability to heal.
- Every healthy cell in your body continues to grow stronger, while your treatment is directed toward

destroying unhealthy cells. Your body wisely knows the difference.

- Each treatment brings you one step closer to recovery. You move forward with courage, patience, and confidence, knowing that healing is taking place every day.

Chemotherapy affects each person differently depending on the type of cancer, the medications used, and the individual's unique response to treatment. While hypnosis is not a substitute for medical care, it is a valuable complementary therapy that can help reduce stress, promote relaxation, ease the perception of treatment-related discomfort, and foster a more positive outlook throughout the chemotherapy journey. Although hypnosis does not treat the cancer itself, it can help patients cope more comfortably and confidently while medical treatment does its important work.

Pain Management

Joanne experienced pain in her body, especially her arms and legs, that limited her from helping her husband, walking, and sleeping. I taught her the control room technique (see Appendix F) to use on herself to minimize the discomfort. With practice, simply closing her eyes, taking a few slow breaths, and imagining herself entering the control room would quickly activate the same feelings of comfort and relaxation, allowing her to reduce discomfort and regain a greater sense of control over her body.

Hypnotic Suggestions for Pain Management

- Each day, you become more comfortable as your body continues to heal and recover.

- You discover that you can gently separate yourself from the discomfort, allowing it to become less important and less noticeable.
- Your mind has the remarkable ability to turn down the volume of discomfort, allowing feelings of comfort and relaxation to become stronger.
- As your body relaxes, tight muscles release, and with that relaxation comes a greater sense of comfort and ease.
- You breathe comfort into the areas that need it most, and with every exhale, you release tension and discomfort.
- You focus your attention on pleasant sensations, peaceful memories, and feelings of well-being, allowing discomfort to fade into the background.
- Each day you notice moments of greater comfort, and those comfortable moments become longer and more frequent.
- You confidently use your hypnosis skills whenever discomfort appears, knowing that you have an effective tool to help yourself feel more comfortable.
- As your comfort increases, you naturally find yourself moving more easily, taking short walks, helping with simple activities, and enjoying more of your day.
- You trust your body's healing process, knowing that every day brings increasing strength, comfort, and hope.

Chapter 16

The Lessons That Shaped Me: Courage, Joy, and Hope

Family stories

Cancer has touched my family in many different ways. My father faced prostate cancer that eventually spread to his bladder. My mother was diagnosed with colon cancer in her nineties. My maternal aunt courageously battled breast cancer in her early fifties. Although their diagnoses were different and each journey unfolded in its own unique way, they all demonstrated remarkable strength, resilience, and grace.

As I watched each of them navigate cancer, I realized there is no single "right" way to face this disease. Some people fight with determination, some with quiet acceptance, and others with an unwavering sense of humor. Each journey is deeply personal, yet each has something to teach us.

The stories that follow are shared with love and gratitude. I hope they remind you that while every cancer experience is different, courage can take many forms, hope can be found in unexpected places, and even in life's most difficult moments, the human spirit has an extraordinary capacity to endure.

My Mother's Story: Joy Until the Very End

My mother was diagnosed with colon cancer in October 2011, shortly after celebrating her ninety-sixth birthday. Looking back, the cancer may have been developing for several years. Beginning in her early nineties, she struggled with constipation and took fiber supplements to help, but she never experienced significant pain.

Because of her age, her physician advised my brother and me not to pursue aggressive treatment. Instead, the focus became keeping her as comfortable as possible.

In March 2012, she was hospitalized with swelling in her legs and increasing discomfort. Until then, she had continued living alone, remarkably independent for someone in her nineties, with a little help from me. After leaving the hospital, she moved to Rosary Hill Home in Hawthorne, New York, where she received compassionate palliative care.

I believe my mother understood that she would not be returning home, although we never had a direct conversation about it. About a month after arriving at Rosary Hill, she quietly asked me to clean out her apartment because she realized she would be spending the rest of her life there. She accepted her circumstances with remarkable grace.

What amazes me most is that cancer never stole her joy.

One of the sisters told me that after my mother's morning shower, they would sometimes dance together around her room.

I can picture it so clearly. That simple image captures exactly who my mother was.

She was also assigned a roommate, a woman in her fifties with advanced bone cancer who was deeply depressed. Over time, my mother's cheerful outlook and infectious spirit seemed to lift her roommate's spirits. Before long, she began participating in activities alongside my mother instead of remaining isolated in her room. My mother had a gift for bringing light wherever she went.

And she never considered herself "old."

She loved telling stories, especially about the time she met "Elvis" at a dinner theater and proudly came home with the scarf he had given her.

One of my favorite memories happened on her ninety-second birthday. I took her to the theater, and the parking lot was filled with buses bringing senior groups. During intermission, she looked around the packed theater, smiled, and loudly announced,

"Wow! Look at all these old people!"

I couldn't help laughing.

"But Mom," I said, "you're ninety-two."

Without missing a beat, she replied,

"Oh no... I don't count."

That was my mother.

She lived with humor, optimism, and a zest for life that never faded, even during her final weeks. She passed away peacefully on May 17, 2012, at the age of ninety-six and a half.

If my father's story taught me courage, my mother's taught me something equally important: our circumstances do not have to define our attitude. Even when facing the end of life, she chose laughter over self-pity, joy over despair, and in doing so, she brought hope not only to herself but to everyone around her.

My mother reminded me that joy doesn't disappear because life becomes difficult. Sometimes it's the very thing that carries us through.

My Father's Story: A Life of Quiet Courage

My father was diagnosed with prostate cancer at the age of sixty-eight. By then, he had finally found a job he truly loved as the assistant superintendent of a Manhattan apartment building. It was a position he had earned after years of hard work in a factory and later in construction when the factory closed. He was a man who believed in honest work, helping others, and never complaining.

About a year before his diagnosis, he began experiencing pain whenever he urinated. Like so many people, he convinced himself it would go away. Unfortunately, it didn't. When he finally sought medical attention, he learned he had prostate cancer that had already spread to his bladder.

His oncologist presented him with two difficult options. One was major surgery to remove his bladder, requiring him to wear a urostomy bag for the rest of his life, with the possibility of living ten years or more. The other was chemotherapy in pill form, which offered a shorter life expectancy but allowed him to avoid such a life-altering operation.

After carefully considering his options, my father made a decision that reflected the way he had always lived his life. He chose the treatment that would allow him to continue living as independently and normally as possible. It wasn't an easy decision, but it was the right one for him.

He took the chemotherapy pills for about a year before the side effects became too difficult to tolerate. Even then, he refused to let cancer define him. Every day, he continued going to work at the apartment building where he had become a favorite among the tenants.

My father was one of those people who could fix almost anything. Whether it was patching a hole in a wall, painting, repairing a leaky faucet, rewiring a lamp, or taking care of countless little jobs, he was always willing to lend a hand. His kindness and dependability earned him the respect and affection of everyone who knew him.

He continued working until he was seventy-one, when the pain from the cancer finally became too much to bear.

One thing always made me smile. Even though he knew I was a hypnotist and understood that hypnosis might help him manage his pain, he wasn't about to let me hypnotize him. That simply wasn't my dad. He was fiercely independent and determined to handle things his own way.

Looking back, I realize that courage doesn't always look dramatic. Sometimes it looks like getting up each morning, going to work, helping other people, making difficult decisions with quiet confidence, and refusing to let illness take away your sense of purpose.

That was my father. And I will always admire the strength, dignity, and determination with which he lived his life.

My father taught me that courage isn't always loud. Sometimes it's simply showing up each day and living according to your values

My Aunt Mary's Story: It's Never Too Late to Change

My mother was very close to her sister, Mary. When Aunt Mary was in her early fifties, she was diagnosed with breast cancer. Although I don't remember what stage her cancer was, I do remember that she underwent a double mastectomy.

Before her diagnosis, Aunt Mary lived a lifestyle that wasn't especially healthy. She smoked about a pack of cigarettes a day, enjoyed an occasional drink, was overweight, ate many processed foods, and got very little exercise.

After her surgery, her oncologist had an honest conversation with her. He explained that while no one could guarantee the future, adopting healthier habits could improve her overall health and give her the best opportunity to live well in the years ahead.

She took those words to heart.

Within a year, Aunt Mary had completely transformed her lifestyle. She quit smoking, stopped drinking, made healthier food choices, lost weight, and made walking a regular part of her daily routine. The changes weren't always easy, but she remained committed to them for the rest of her life.

Whether those lifestyle changes added years to her life, no one can say for certain. What I do know is that she enjoyed many healthy, active years afterward and lived to the remarkable age of ninety-three.

Her story reminds me that a cancer diagnosis can sometimes become a turning point. While we cannot change yesterday, we can choose what we do today. Every healthy choice we make is an investment in our future, and it is never too late to begin.

Aunt Mary showed me that it's never too late to make changes that support your health and well-being.

Final Thoughts

The stories in this chapter are more than memories of the people I loved. Each one taught me something different about facing cancer. My father showed me quiet courage and the importance of making the treatment decision that was right for him. My mother reminded me that even in life's final chapter, joy, laughter, and kindness can still flourish. My Aunt Mary demonstrated that a cancer diagnosis can become a powerful motivation to make healthier choices and embrace a new way of living.

Although their paths were different, each of them left me with lessons that have stayed with me throughout my own cancer journey. It is my hope that their stories will offer you encouragement as you travel your own path, reminding you that there is no one right way to face cancer—only the way that is right for you.

Chapter 17

Voices of Hope

Lessons from Fellow Survivors

Although this book began with my own cancer journey, I knew from the very beginning that I didn't want it to be only my story. Every cancer diagnosis is unique, but the emotions we experience—fear, uncertainty, hope, determination, and gratitude—are remarkably similar. I wanted you to hear from others who have traveled this road because each survivor has something valuable to teach us.

The stories in this section are shared by survivors of different ages, with different or similar types of cancer, different treatments, and different life experiences. Some faced surgery, chemotherapy, radiation, or hormone therapy. Others encountered unexpected challenges or long-term side effects. Yet each found the strength to move forward in his or her own way. While no two journeys are exactly alike, I hope you'll discover that you are never alone in what you're feeling.

My wish is that as you read these stories, you'll find pieces of yourself in them. Perhaps one survivor's courage will inspire you. Another's honesty will reassure you that your fears are normal. Someone else's experience may offer practical ideas or simply remind you that healing is possible, even when the path seems difficult. Most of all, I hope these stories give you hope.

I am deeply grateful to each person who generously shared their cancer journey for this book. It takes courage to revisit such a personal chapter of life, and I am honored that they trusted me with their stories. To protect their privacy, most of the names used in these pages have been changed, but the experiences, emotions, and lessons they share are genuine. My heartfelt thanks to each of them for helping make this book a source of comfort and encouragement for others.

As you finish each story, you'll find a brief section called **" A Rainbow of Hope."** These are the survivor's own words—or the message that best captures the heart of their experience. My hope is that these simple thoughts will remind you that even after life's fiercest storms, hope can still shine through, one rainbow at a time.

Babs' Story

Babs was only 46 years old and newly married when a routine mammogram changed the course of her life. It was her very first mammogram, and although she felt perfectly healthy, it revealed calcifications that required further testing. A biopsy confirmed what no one wants to hear—she had Stage 1 ductal carcinoma in situ (DCIS), a very early form of breast cancer.

The diagnosis came as a complete shock. Married for only six months, Babs remembers wondering why cancer had entered her life just as she was beginning this exciting new chapter. Like so many people, her first thoughts were of death and the uncertainty of what lay ahead.

After carefully discussing her options with her physicians, Babs chose to have a mastectomy rather than a lumpectomy followed by chemotherapy and radiation. She wanted the treatment that gave her the greatest peace of mind and allowed her to move forward with confidence. Reconstruction began at the same time as her surgery, although the process brought its own challenges. Another unexpected challenge came during Babs' breast reconstruction. Before her surgery, she had always had small breasts and was comfortable with her body. Unfortunately, implants in her original size were not available, so she had no choice but to have the next larger size implanted in both breasts to maintain symmetry. Although she would have preferred to remain her original size, she gradually learned to accept this unexpected change as just another part of her cancer journey. Looking back, she smiles when she says that her husband was never "a breast man." What mattered most to him was that she was healthy and still by his side. His unconditional love and acceptance helped reassure her that she was far more than the changes cancer had made to her body. She vividly remembers the discomfort caused by adhesive bandages and the strange muscle spasms she experienced as the tissue expanders gradually stretched her skin, describing the sensation as feeling like "seltzer bubbles" beneath the surface.

One of the most difficult side effects Babs experienced while taking tamoxifen was frequent hot flashes. In the beginning, they occurred almost every hour and continued throughout the four years she took the medication. Even today, she still experiences an occasional hot flash. As a musician who performs with her band, she has learned to adapt by dressing in layers. It isn't unusual for her to put on a sweater before a performance, only to remove it in the middle of a gig when a hot flash suddenly strikes. Like so many other aspects of her cancer journey, she has learned to adjust with grace, humor, and resilience.

One of the blessings throughout her journey was the confidence she had in her medical team. Her surgeon inspired trust from the very beginning, and Babs believes that feeling secure in her physicians played an important role in her emotional healing. She also drew tremendous strength from her husband, family, and friends, especially those who had faced cancer themselves. Although support groups were never the right fit for her, one-on-one conversations with fellow survivors reminded her that she was not alone.

Babs' surgery took place on September 11, 2000. As the one-year anniversary approached, she and a close friend planned to celebrate what she considered an important milestone—one year cancer-free. Instead, their plans were abruptly overshadowed by the tragic events of September 11, 2001. What was meant to be a day of personal celebration became a day of unimaginable national sorrow. Since then, September 11 has held two very different meanings for Babs: a deeply personal reminder of her own cancer journey and a day forever etched in our nation's history. Looking back more than twenty-five years later, Babs sees cancer as an experience that transformed her life in unexpected ways.

A Native American pipe carrier once shared a perspective that has stayed with her ever since. He told her that she was giving a small physical piece of herself back to the Creator in exchange for a much greater spiritual gift. That simple thought helped her find meaning in an experience that had once seemed only frightening.

Today, Babs approaches life differently. The little frustrations that once seemed overwhelming rarely bother her anymore because, as she says, "It's not breast cancer." Surviving cancer has given her greater confidence, deeper gratitude, and a new appreciation for every day. She returned to performing only ten days after surgery, a reflection of the determination that has always been part of her character.

When someone is newly diagnosed, Babs offers reassuring words born from experience. "It's not a death sentence," she tells them. She also encourages people to let go of guilt. None of us can know why cancer develops, and blaming ourselves only adds another burden to carry. Most importantly, she promises that there will come a day when cancer is no longer the first thought upon waking each morning. Life gradually returns, hope grows stronger, and healing becomes about much more than the body.

As I listened to Babs share her story, I was struck by her remarkable perspective. Her experience reminds us that healing is not only about surviving cancer but also about discovering unexpected strength, renewed purpose, and a deeper appreciation for life itself.

As a hypnotist, I also thought about how hypnosis could have supported Babs throughout different parts of her journey. I would have helped her adjust emotionally to the changes in her body following reconstruction, allowing her to develop acceptance and comfort with her new implants. Hypnosis could also have been used to help manage the challenges of menopause symptoms, including the frequent hot flashes she experienced while taking tamoxifen. In addition, I would have taught her the **Control Room Technique** (described in the Appendix), a powerful self-hypnosis tool that can help individuals change their perception of discomfort and develop a greater sense of control over pain. While hypnosis does not change what has happened, it can provide another resource for coping, relaxation, and confidence during the healing process.

A Rainbow of Hope from Babs

"There will come a day when cancer is no longer the first thing you think about. That day will come."

Dominique's Story

At 62 years old, Dominique's life changed with four words she never expected to hear: *You have uterine cancer.* Looking back, she realized that her body had been trying to tell her something long before the diagnosis. About a year earlier, she began experiencing vaginal bleeding. She knew it wasn't menstruation—she had gone through menopause several years before—but instead of making an appointment with her doctor, she found herself in denial. Like many people, she was afraid of what she might hear and hoped the problem would simply go away.

Nearly a year passed before Dominique finally sought medical care. After a series of tests, her doctor confirmed that she had uterine cancer. She was devastated. Shocked and overwhelmed, she remembers asking, "Why me?" Accepting the diagnosis was one of the hardest parts of her journey. Fortunately, her cancer was slow growing. She underwent surgery to remove her uterus, followed by three rounds of radiation treatment. Today, she feels grateful that she has no lasting side effects from her treatment.

Throughout her cancer journey, Dominique leaned heavily on her faith in God. Prayer became her source of strength, and knowing that family, friends, and members of her faith community were praying for her brought comfort during some of her darkest days. She also found tremendous support from her friends, who stood beside her when she needed them most.

Cancer changed Dominique's outlook on life. Today, she embraces each day with gratitude and purpose. She enjoys taking trips, going to the movies, meeting friends for lunch or dinner, reading, playing games on Facebook, and attending a weekly Tai Chi class. One simple sentence captures the way she now lives: **"Tomorrow is not promised."** Rather than putting off the things that bring her joy, she makes the most of each day.

Dominique also has an important message for others. If something doesn't seem right, don't hesitate to see your doctor. Don't let fear or denial keep you from getting answers. Early action can make all the difference.

As a hypnotist, I couldn't help but think about how hypnosis might have supported Dominique emotionally. I would have helped her release any self-blame she may have carried for waiting so long to seek medical care. Instead of focusing on the delay, I would encourage her to recognize the courage it took to finally make that appointment. I would also reinforce that accepting help from others is not a sign of weakness but a gift that allows family and friends to express their love and support. Healing involves not only caring for the body but also extending compassion to ourselves.

A Rainbow of Hope from Dominique

"Tomorrow is not promised. Live today with gratitude, joy, and hope."

Paulette's Story

Paulette, a 57-year-old administrator, had always been faithful about getting her annual mammogram every April. One year, however, life became busy, and she postponed it until

September. Looking back, that delay may have been a blessing in disguise. After reviewing her mammogram, the radiologist recommended a sonogram, followed by a biopsy. On October 1, 2024, Paulette received the phone call confirming she had Stage I breast cancer.

The radiologist later explained that because her cancer was slow growing and non-aggressive, it might not have been visible had she kept her original April appointment.

Paulette remembers exactly where she was when she received the call. She had just arrived home from work and was preparing dinner. She cried when she heard the diagnosis, but after a few moments, she gathered herself together and finished preparing the meal. When her husband came home, they quietly ate dinner together before she told him the news. Looking back, she describes her immediate response as going into "survivor mode." She wasn't interested in asking, "Why me?" She simply wanted the surgeon to do whatever was necessary to get the cancer out of her body.

Because her cancer was not aggressive, her surgeon reassured her that it was safe to wait until surgery could be scheduled. On December 16, she underwent a lumpectomy on her left breast. Afterwards, the tissue was sent for an Oncotype DX test, which estimates the likelihood of cancer recurrence and helps determine whether chemotherapy is beneficial. Waiting nearly three weeks for those results was one of the most difficult parts of her entire journey. During that time, devastating wildfires were spreading across California, where she thought the specialized laboratory performing the test was located. Paulette worried that the fires might destroy the laboratory and her tissue sample before the results could be completed. Thankfully, the laboratory was located outside the affected area, and the results arrived safely. Based on her score, chemotherapy was recommended to significantly reduce her risk of recurrence.

She received eight rounds of chemotherapy every two weeks through an IV, followed by fifteen radiation treatments over three weeks. Fortunately, nausea was well controlled with medication, and by eating simple, bland foods she maintained her appetite throughout treatment. Her greatest challenge during chemotherapy was overwhelming fatigue, while radiation left her with aching bones.

One memory from surgery day still stands out. While waiting to be taken into the operating room, she found herself in a small room with her husband, both sets of parents, and everyone anxiously waiting. Although she appreciated their love and support, all she really wanted was a few quiet moments alone with her thoughts. It reminded her that caregivers often cope with cancer differently than the patient.

Throughout treatment, Paulette continued working with the support of understanding supervisors and coworkers. During chemotherapy weeks, she rested during the first week and worked from home during the second. She also chose to share parts of her journey on Facebook, always posting messages filled with hope and optimism. When she completed radiation, she proudly shared a photograph of herself ringing the hospital's cancer bell.

Today, Paulette walks nearly 10,000 steps each day, follows a Mediterranean diet, and is grateful for the support of her husband, family, and friends. She says her husband may have been even more frightened than she was. Although she still lives with the fear of recurrence and describes herself as having "posttraumatic stress from cancer," she refuses to let fear define her future.

Her advice to others is practical and heartfelt: never skip your mammograms, listen to your body, ask questions, and become an active participant in your own care. Most importantly, trust your medical team. If you don't feel comfortable with your doctors, keep looking until you find the ones you do trust.

As a hypnotist, I thought about how hypnosis could have helped Paulette during several points in her journey. While waiting for the Oncotype DX results, self-hypnosis could have eased the anxiety of uncertainty and the frightening "what if" thoughts that filled those three weeks. During chemotherapy, hypnosis could have helped manage fatigue, promote relaxation, and support restful sleep. As she continues moving forward, self-hypnosis can also become a valuable tool for quieting the understandable fear of recurrence, allowing her to focus more fully on living each day rather than worrying about tomorrow.

A Rainbow of Hope from Paulette

"Listen to your body. Stay positive, ask questions, trust your doctors, and never take your health for granted."

Taylor's Story

Taylor was 61 years old when a single, subtle sign changed her life. One day she noticed the toilet paper was pink after she wiped. It happened only once and then disappeared. Two weeks later, it happened again. Deep down, she knew something was not right. She immediately made an appointment with her OB/GYN, who performed a biopsy in June 2024. On July 7, Taylor received the phone call that no one wants to hear—she had endometrial uterine cancer. Her oncologist explained that it was the most aggressive type.

Taylor's first reaction was fear. She cried and admitted that thoughts of dying flooded her mind. But she has always been someone who faces problems head-on. After allowing herself time to absorb the diagnosis, she gathered her strength and focused on what she could control. She consulted two surgeons before deciding on the one she trusted most. Looking back, Taylor encourages others to do the same. Feeling comfortable and confident in your medical team is an important part of your healing journey.

Her surgery was scheduled for July 26. She underwent a complete hysterectomy along with the removal of 33 abdominal lymph nodes. Following surgery, she received six rounds of chemotherapy, each lasting about five hours and scheduled every three weeks on a Friday. Working as a dental receptionist, Taylor planned her treatments so she could recover over the weekend and return to work on Monday. Aside from losing her hair two weeks after beginning chemotherapy, her most difficult side effect was severe pain in her legs for several days after each treatment. By Wednesday, however, the pain would subside, allowing her to continue with her normal routine. She wore a wig after losing her hair and smiled as she shared that although she had always had straight hair, it grew back curly. At first she wasn't happy about the change, but eventually she learned to embrace her new look.

Before her diagnosis, Taylor faithfully attended water aerobics classes. Because she needed a chemotherapy port, she had to give them up temporarily, something she greatly missed. Today, she is happy to be back in the pool.

Throughout her journey, Taylor drew strength from her family, friends, and her unwavering faith in God. She promised God that if He brought her through this experience, she would attend Mass every day. Since she does not drive, she faithfully watches Mass online each morning at 7:00 a.m., or in the evening if she misses the morning service. She also found comfort in the many prayers offered on her behalf, believing they lifted her spirits during her darkest moments. Her philosophy became simple: if she could lift her head off the pillow each morning, she was going to get up, go to work, and keep living her life.

Today, Taylor eats healthier, gets more sleep, and treasures every day. One thing she wishes she had at the beginning of her diagnosis was someone who had already walked the same path. Now she has become that person for another woman with the same diagnosis. The woman affectionately calls Taylor "the angel on my shoulder," a title that speaks volumes about the comfort and hope she now offers others.

Taylor's advice is heartfelt: trust your doctors, lean on your faith, take one day at a time, and live life to the fullest. As a hypnotist, I also thought about how hypnosis could have eased some of her journey. I would have taught her self-hypnosis to help manage the leg pain she experienced after chemotherapy and introduced her to the **Control Room Technique** (described in the Appendix), a powerful way to reduce discomfort by learning to influence how the mind interprets pain. Sometimes the greatest gift we can give ourselves is learning that while we may not be able to control every circumstance, we can learn to influence how we respond to it.

A Rainbow of Hope from Taylor

"If I could lift my head off the pillow, I got up, went to work, and lived my life."

Tammy's Story

Tammy was 64 years old when a routine mammogram on June 6, 2010, changed her life. The radiologist noticed a small area that didn't look quite right. Additional testing confirmed it was Stage I breast cancer.

Like so many others, Tammy's first reaction was shock. But after the initial disbelief, an unexpected thought crossed her mind: *"Who's going to take care of my dog if I die?"* Looking back, she smiles at that memory. It was a reminder that even in life's most frightening moments, our minds often focus on the people—and pets—we love most.

Tammy underwent a lumpectomy, but her journey wasn't quite finished. A week later, her doctors recommended testing her lymph nodes. After injecting dye to identify the sentinel nodes, they removed five lymph nodes for examination. Thankfully, every one of them was cancer-free.

One thing that stands out about Tammy is her determination to keep living her life. She had surgery on a Friday and was back to work as the director of a school by Monday. Following surgery, she completed seven weeks of radiation treatments, Monday through Friday. Her appointments were scheduled for 7:00 each morning, allowing her to arrive at work by 8:00. Afterwards, she faithfully took hormone therapy for five years, missing only two doses during that entire time—and only because she accidentally fell asleep before taking them.

Although Tammy has no close family nearby, she quickly discovered the importance of asking for help. She needed someone to drive her to both surgeries. Several friends were unable to do so, but she didn't give up. She kept asking until an acquaintance who lived twelve miles away willingly offered to help, getting up at 5:30 each morning to take her to the hospital. That simple act of kindness left a lasting impression. Tammy believes that the support of friends can make all the difference during a cancer journey.

Her faith in God also sustained her. She prayed throughout her treatment and continues to pray today. She believes faith is not something we turn to only during times of crisis but something that remains part of our lives after our prayers have been answered.

Sixteen years later, Tammy remains cancer-free. Along the way, she has faced other health challenges, including sepsis, a knee replacement, and a hip replacement. Yet she refuses to slow down. When her physical therapy sessions ended, she joined a gym so she could continue exercising on her own. Her philosophy is simple: keep moving. Stay active in both body and mind.

Tammy's advice is practical and inspiring. Trust your doctors. Accept help when it is offered. Stay active. Most importantly, make up your mind that you are going to get back to living your life as soon as possible. Cancer may change your life, but it does not have to define it.

As a hypnotist, I thought about how hypnosis could have supported Tammy throughout her journey. Self-hypnosis could have helped reduce the stress surrounding surgery, encouraged comfort during radiation treatments, and reinforced her already strong determination to heal. I also would have used hypnosis to strengthen her confidence, encourage relaxation, and support her commitment to remaining active. Her positive attitude became one of her greatest strengths, and hypnosis could have served as another valuable tool to reinforce that resilient mindset.

🌈 A Rainbow of Hope from Tammy

"Stay active. Trust your doctors. Lean on your faith, accept help from others, and make up your mind that you're going to get back to living your life."

Larry's Story

I have known Larry for nearly forty years, not only as a dear friend but also as a respected colleague in the hypnosis profession. Now 84 years old, Larry has maintained a hypnosis practice in Chicago for more than fifty years. Throughout his life, he has been known for his positive attitude and calm approach to life's challenges. Cancer had touched his family before—his mother was a cancer survivor, and his brother was diagnosed with cancer around the same time Larry received his own diagnosis.

Larry's cancer journey began in March 2020, just as the COVID lockdown was taking hold. His only symptom was a small bump on his neck. Because of the pandemic, finding doctors and getting timely treatment became an unexpected challenge. When he was finally diagnosed with throat cancer, his response was surprisingly calm. Instead of asking, "Why me?" he simply thought, "Okay...now what?" He believed that worrying wouldn't change the situation and trusted that somehow everything would work out.

His first physician told him the tumor was quite large. Before moving forward, Larry visited an Asian holistic practitioner who treated him with herbs and believed the tumor would shrink. When he sought a second surgical opinion, the surgeon confirmed that it had indeed become smaller.

Larry underwent nine weeks of chemotherapy and radiation. As a hypnotist whose livelihood depended on his voice, he naturally worried about the effects of treatment. Years earlier, surgery to remove cysts from his vocal cords had left him unable to speak for two weeks. Fortunately, this time his voice remained strong, although he wisely took a year away from his practice to focus on healing.

Support came from every direction. His family, friends, neighbors, and healthcare team were always there for him. Even his mail carrier checked on him every day. His oncologist became not only an outstanding physician but also a friend who developed an interest in hypnosis. Larry also relied on the same tool he had taught his clients for decades. He created hypnosis recordings for himself and listened to them every day, using hypnosis to bring peace, relaxation, and confidence throughout his treatment.

Today, Larry continues to enjoy life by eating healthier, taking daily walks with his beloved dog, Rosie, and appreciating each day. Chemotherapy left him with neuropathy in his feet and fingertips, requiring him to be cautious when walking and when holding objects. Radiation also damaged his teeth and gums, and he is preparing for oral surgery and dental implants. Yet these challenges have never diminished his optimism.

Larry's advice to anyone facing cancer is both simple and profound: think positively, take one day at a time, and live in the present instead of letting anxiety about tomorrow steal today's peace. Listen carefully to your doctors, but don't allow discouraging words or limiting beliefs to define your future. He often recalls an old television commercial that said, "If you want to know about the car, ask the person who drives one." Likewise, he encourages newly diagnosed patients to talk with someone who has traveled the same road. Above all, Larry believes that if you face cancer with hope, determination, and confidence, you can come through the experience not only as a survivor but as a stronger, wiser, and more grateful person.

A Rainbow of Hope from Larry

"Take one day at a time, live in the moment, and believe everything will work out."

What These Survivors Taught Me

When I began interviewing these remarkable survivors, I expected to hear different stories. Different diagnoses. Different treatments. Different outcomes.

What I didn't expect was that, despite all their differences, they shared so many of the same lessons.

Babs reminded me that cancer is not a death sentence. She taught us that healing also means accepting changes in our bodies and trusting that those who love us see far beyond physical appearance.

Dominique reminded us not to ignore our body's warning signs. She also showed us that faith, friendship, and gratitude can help us discover joy again because tomorrow truly is not promised.

Paulette demonstrated the importance of becoming an active participant in our own care. She reminded us to ask questions, trust our instincts, and never take our health—or our annual mammograms—for granted.

Taylor showed extraordinary determination. She faced an aggressive cancer without allowing it to define her. Today, she has become the very person she once wished she had beside her—an encouraging voice for someone beginning the same journey.

Tammy taught us that healing doesn't stop when treatment ends. Sixteen years after her diagnosis, she continues to embrace life with gratitude, faith, and determination, reminding us to stay active, accept help, and never stop moving forward.

Larry reminded us that attitude matters. His message to live in the moment, believe in yourself, and seek wisdom from those who have already traveled this road beautifully captures the spirit of every survivor in this chapter.

Although their stories are different, they all discovered something remarkable. Cancer changed them, but it did not define them. Each found strength they never knew they possessed. Each accepted help from others. Each discovered hope beyond fear.

Different people. Different cancers. Different journeys. Yet every one of them discovered hope after the storm.

My hope is that somewhere within these pages, you found a survivor whose story spoke directly to your heart. Perhaps you recognized yourself in their fears, their determination, their faith, or their resilience. If so, remember that their journey is living proof that there can be life after cancer.

As you continue your own journey, may you carry with you not only their stories but also their hope. And may you discover, in your own time and in your own way, the rainbow that waits after every storm.

Chapter 18

Finding Your Rainbow

Surviving—and Thriving—After the Storm

When I first heard the words, *"You have cancer,"* I could never have imagined writing this final chapter. Like so many people, I wondered what lay ahead. Would I survive? How difficult would treatment be? Would I ever feel like myself again? At the time, the future seemed hidden behind dark storm clouds, and it was impossible to see beyond them.

Today, I know something I couldn't fully appreciate then. Storms do pass. Life may never look exactly the way it did before cancer, but it can still be filled with hope, purpose, laughter, love, and joy. That has been the promise of this book from the very beginning. My hope has never been simply to tell my story, but to reassure you that, although cancer changes your life, it does not have to define the rest of it.

Throughout these pages, I've shared my own journey—from finding the lump in my breast, through surgery, chemotherapy, radiation, and learning to live with lymphedema. Along the way, I discovered that healing involves much more than treating the body. It means caring for your emotional well-being, finding ways to calm your mind, accepting help when you need it, and learning to live one day at a time. I learned that hope isn't something we discover after everything is over. Hope is something we choose every day, even while walking through uncertainty.

One of the greatest blessings throughout my journey was my husband, Robert. From the day of my diagnosis, he walked beside me every step of the way. He accompanied me to appointments, listened carefully as doctors explained treatment options, and often remembered details I had forgotten. During chemotherapy, he used hypnosis to help me remain calm and reduce nausea. Later, when lymphedema became part of my life, he learned lymphatic massage, helped me put on my nighttime compression garment, and never complained about the extra responsibilities cancer had placed on both of us. More importantly, he reminded me every day that I wasn't facing cancer alone. His love, patience, and unwavering support became an important part of my healing.

As meaningful as my own story has been, I wanted this book to include the experiences of others because no two cancer journeys are exactly alike. My family's stories taught me resilience long before I ever received my own diagnosis. My father chose quality of life and continued living with dignity and purpose despite his illness. My mother demonstrated remarkable grace during the final chapter of her life, and my Aunt Mary showed that it is never too late to make healthy lifestyle changes that can positively influence our future. Each of them taught me something different about courage, acceptance, and perseverance.

The survivors who generously shared their stories reinforced those same lessons. Although their cancers, treatments, and circumstances were different, their journeys shared many common threads. They leaned on family and friends, trusted their medical teams, found strength they never knew they possessed, and gradually discovered that life could once again include laughter, travel, meaningful relationships, faith, and new dreams. Many told me that cancer changed them forever—not because it made them weaker, but because it revealed strengths they never knew they had.

Perhaps that is one of cancer's greatest paradoxes. None of us would ever choose this journey, yet many survivors discover greater compassion, deeper gratitude, stronger relationships, and a renewed appreciation for everyday life. That doesn't make cancer a blessing, but it does remind us that something beautiful can still grow from one of life's most difficult experiences.

If you are reading this shortly after your diagnosis, you may still feel as though you are standing in the middle of your own storm. Some days you may feel hopeful; other days you may feel frightened, discouraged, angry, or exhausted. Every one of those feelings is normal. You do not have to solve every problem today. You do not have to face your entire journey all at once. Simply take the next step, then the one after that. Trust your medical team. Accept help from those who love you. Be gentle with yourself, and remember that healing is rarely a straight line. There will be good days and difficult days, but both are part of the journey.

I also hope that the hypnosis techniques you've learned throughout this book become valuable companions along the way. While hypnosis is not a treatment for cancer itself, it can help quiet fear, reduce stress, encourage relaxation, improve comfort, and remind you that your mind can become one of your greatest allies during treatment and recovery. It became an important part of my own journey, and I hope it offers you the same sense of peace and confidence it brought me.

Looking back now, I realize that cancer changed many things about my life, but it never changed who I was. Instead, it deepened my appreciation for ordinary moments, strengthened my relationships, increased my compassion for others, and reminded me never to take a single day for granted. It also inspired me to write this book with the hope that no one facing cancer would ever feel quite so alone.

If there is one message I hope you carry with you after closing this book, it is this: cancer is something that happened to you—it is not who you are. You are still the same person with hopes, dreams, talents, people who love you, and a future that continues to unfold. Your diagnosis does not define your worth, your purpose, or your ability to experience happiness again.

One day, perhaps sooner than you can imagine, you may find yourself encouraging someone who has just begun the journey you are now walking. You may discover that your experience, your compassion, and your willingness to simply listen become exactly what another person needs. That is how hope continues—one survivor reaching out to another, one act of kindness at a time.

When I chose the title *The Rainbow After the Storm*, it wasn't because I believed cancer was easy or that every day would be filled with sunshine. I chose it because rainbows only appear after storms. They remind us that even after the darkest skies, beauty still exists. Hope still exists. Life still exists.

As you close this book and continue your own journey, I hope you will remember that no storm lasts forever. There may be days when the clouds seem heavy and the path ahead feels uncertain, but keep moving forward one step at a time. Lean on those who love you, trust your medical team, care for both your body and your mind, and never lose sight of hope. Those simple steps carried me through my own journey, and they have carried countless other survivors through theirs.

When I began writing this book, I promised you that there could be a rainbow after the storm. Now, after sharing my story, my family's stories, and the journeys of so many courageous survivors, I hope you believe that promise too. We are living proof that it is possible not only to survive cancer, but to thrive after it.

My wish for you is that one day you will look back and realize that this storm did not define your life—it revealed your strength. And as the clouds begin to part, may you discover your own rainbow, filled with hope, healing, renewed purpose, and the quiet joy of knowing that beautiful things can still grow after life's greatest storms.

How to Use the Self-Hypnosis Scripts

The appendices contain a collection of self-hypnosis scripts that you can use whenever you need them. Each script is designed to help you cope with a different aspect of your cancer journey—from reducing stress and managing fear to improving sleep, increasing comfort, and strengthening hope.

The **Progressive Relaxation** exercise is the starting point for all of these scripts EXCEPT The Self Hypnosis Exercise. Think of it as the doorway into hypnosis. It helps you relax your body, quiet your mind, and enter a comfortable state of focused attention where the suggestions that follow can become more meaningful and effective. Each time you use one of the self-hypnosis scripts, Appendices C to F begin with the Progressive Relaxation exercise.

Once you are comfortably in hypnosis, you have several options. You may ask a trusted friend, family member, or caregiver to slowly read the script to you. You may gently open your eyes—yes, you really can open your eyes and remain in hypnosis—and read the script yourself. Or you may record the script in your own voice and listen to the recording whenever you wish.

Many people are surprised to learn that hypnosis is not sleep. Rather, it is a natural state of focused attention and relaxed awareness. Simply choose the method that feels most comfortable for you. There is no "right" or "wrong" way to use these exercises. The goal is to relax, absorb the positive suggestions, and allow your mind and body to work together in support of your healing, comfort, and overall well-being.

A few words of caution: Do not practice these exercises when you are overly tired, as you may simply drift off to sleep before receiving the full benefit of the suggestions. If you record the scripts in your own voice, never listen to them while driving, operating machinery, or engaging in any activity that requires your full attention. Instead, use them only when you can relax safely and without interruption.

In Brief

Before using any appendices C-F

- Begin with the **Progressive Relaxation** exercise.
- Then choose the method that works best for you:
    - Ask someone you trust to read the script aloud.
    - Record the script in your own voice and play it back.
    - Enter hypnosis with Progressive Relaxation, gently open your eyes, and read the script yourself while remaining in hypnosis.

How to Use the Self-Hypnosis Suggestion Exercise

Unlike the longer self-hypnosis scripts in this appendix, C – F this brief exercise is designed to be personalized. As you read each chapter in this book, you will find a number of short self-hypnosis suggestions related to that topic. Before beginning this exercise, choose two or three of the suggestions that are most meaningful to you.

You do NOT need to complete Progressive Relaxation exercise.

Start with I feel calm...I feel relaxed... etc and when you reach the point in the script marked **Pause Here**, slowly repeat your selected suggestions several times. Take your time. Allow each suggestion to become comfortable, meaningful, and believable as you gently absorb it. You may repeat the same suggestion several times before moving on to the next, or alternate between two or three suggestions—whatever feels most natural to you.

When you have finished repeating your selected suggestions, simply continue with the remainder of the Self-Hypnosis Suggestion Exercise.

As your needs change throughout your cancer journey, you can return to this exercise and choose different suggestions from other chapters. In this way, one simple self-hypnosis exercise can be used again and again to help you address the challenges you are facing at that moment.

Pause Here

Slowly repeat the two or three self-hypnosis suggestions you selected from the chapter you are working on. Repeat each suggestion several times, allowing the words to become comfortable, natural, and meaningful. Continue for as long as you wish. When you are ready, continue with the remainder of the exercise.

Remember, these exercises are not about doing hypnosis perfectly. They are simply tools to help you relax, quiet your mind, and tap into your own inner resources for healing. The more often you practice, the more natural and effective the process is likely to become.

Appendix A

Progressive Muscle Relaxation for Self-Hypnosis

Find a comfortable position, either sitting in a supportive chair or lying down. Allow your hands to rest comfortably, and gently close your eyes.

Take a slow, deep breath in...and exhale slowly. Again...breathe in deeply...and let the tension melt away as you exhale.

One more deep breath...and as you breathe out, allow yourself to settle into a state of peaceful relaxation.

Now bring your attention to the **top of your head**. Imagine a wave of warmth and relaxation beginning there, gently spreading across your scalp. Feel every tiny muscle relaxing completely.

Allow that feeling to move down to your **forehead**. Smooth away any lines or tension. Your forehead becomes soft, loose, and comfortable.

Now relax the muscles around your **eyes**. Your eyelids become pleasantly heavy as the tiny muscles surrounding your eyes let go completely.

Relax your **cheeks**, allowing them to soften.

Relax your **jaw**. If your teeth are touching, allow them to separate slightly. Let your jaw hang comfortably loose.

Relax your **tongue**, your **mouth**, and all the muscles of your **face**.

Now allow the relaxation to flow into your **neck**, releasing any tightness or stiffness you may be carrying there.

The feeling continues into your **shoulders**. Imagine the weight of the day simply melting away. Your shoulders become loose, relaxed, and comfortable.

Now relax your **upper arms**, your **elbows**, your **forearms**, your **wrists**, your **hands**, and finally each of your **fingers**. Both arms now feel comfortably relaxed and pleasantly heavy.

Allow the relaxation to spread into your **upper back** and **chest**. Your breathing becomes slow, gentle, and effortless.

Relax your **mid-back** and **lower back**, allowing those muscles to loosen and soften with every breath.

Now let your **abdomen** relax completely. There is no need to hold in your stomach. Simply allow those muscles to become loose and comfortable.

Feel the relaxation moving into your **hips** and **pelvis**, releasing any remaining tension.

Now relax your **thighs**, allowing the large muscles to become loose and comfortable.

The relaxation flows into your **knees**, then down into your **calves**, releasing every bit of tightness.

Relax your **ankles**, your **feet**, and finally each of your **toes**.

From the top of your head to the tips of your toes, every muscle in your body is comfortably relaxed.

Take a moment to enjoy this wonderful feeling of peace and comfort.

As you continue to breathe slowly and naturally, imagine this feeling of relaxation becoming twice as deep with every breath.

In this deeply relaxed state, your mind is calm, your body is comfortable, and your unconscious mind is open to accepting positive suggestions that support your health, healing, and well-being.

Remain here for as long as you wish, enjoying this peaceful feeling.

When you are ready to return to full awareness, take a deep breath. Gently move your fingers and toes. Stretch if you like, and when you are ready, open your eyes, bringing back with you a wonderful feeling of relaxation, comfort, and renewed energy.

Appendix B

SELF-HYPNOSIS SUGGESTION

INSTRUCTIONS: This exercise takes only a few minutes to accomplish and should be practiced at least twice a day. You may keep your eyes closed or open. The pauses are indicated by : . . .

DO THIS EXERCISE SLOWLY.

NEVER practice this while you are driving or operating any type of machinery. You may say the following suggestions to yourself quietly or out loud. All it requires is your concentration. If possible, commit these suggestions to memory.

I feel calm . . . . I feel relaxed . . . . I feel in control . . . I am calm . . . . I am relaxed . . . . I am in control . . . . I feel safe . . . . I feel secure . . . . I am letting go . . . . As I let go, all my muscle groups begin to relax . . . . I feel calm . . . . I feel relaxed . . . . I feel in control . . . .

As my muscle groups relax, a beam of sunlight enters my body, and spreads relaxation throughout my body . . . . It rids me of all negative thoughts and feelings . . . . leaving me with only positive thoughts and feelings . . . . I feel calm . . . . I feel relaxed . . . . I feel in control . . . .

My subconscious mind is now open to receive the helpful and beneficial suggestions I'm about to give myself. . . .

Pause Here

Slowly repeat the two or three self-hypnosis suggestions you selected from the chapter you are working on. Repeat each suggestion several times, allowing the words to become comfortable, natural, and meaningful. Continue for as long as you wish. When you are ready, continue with the remainder of the exercise.

I feel calm . . . . I feel relaxed . . . . I feel in control . . . . I am calm . . . . I am relaxed . . . . I am in control . . . .

Count forward from one to three and open your eyes

Appendix C

The Garden Gate Technique Living Well with Lymphedema

Begin this exercise after completing the Progressive Relaxation script.

Before you begin, find a comfortable position where you can relax without interruption for the next several minutes. Take a slow, easy breath in... and gently let it out. With each breath, allow your body to become a little more relaxed and your mind a little quieter.

Now imagine yourself walking through the most beautiful garden you have ever seen.

The sun is warm but gentle. A light breeze brushes across your face, and you hear the peaceful sounds of birds singing nearby. Every flower is vibrant, every tree healthy and strong. You notice how peaceful this garden feels.

As you continue walking, you discover that beneath the flowers and trees is an irrigation system that quietly carries water throughout the entire garden. Tiny streams flow through small channels, bringing nourishment wherever it is needed.

Think of these channels as representing your lymphatic system.

The water represents the lymph fluid that normally moves gently through your body, supporting health and balance.

As you follow one of the small streams, you notice a series of little garden gates along the irrigation channels. Each gate is designed to open easily, allowing the water to continue flowing naturally from one section of the garden to the next.

Walk to the first gate.

With the gentlest touch, it swings open effortlessly.

The water begins flowing smoothly through the channel.

A little farther along, you come to another gate.

Again, it opens easily.

The water continues moving peacefully along its natural pathway.

One by one, each garden gate opens with ease, allowing the water to continue its quiet journey until it reaches the larger stream that carries it onward.

There is no force.

No struggle.

No rushing.

Only a calm, steady movement.

As you continue breathing slowly and comfortably, imagine your own body responding to this peaceful image.

Picture your lymphatic system working together with the care you receive from your healthcare team, your gentle movement, your compression garments, your self-care, and your relaxation.

Allow yourself to imagine healthy flow...

comfortable movement...

and a growing sense of balance.

Whether or not you actually feel anything changing is unimportant.

Simply allowing yourself to experience this peaceful image can help quiet the mind, relax the body, and strengthen your commitment to caring for yourself.

Take another slow breath.

As you exhale, silently repeat:

"Every day I care for my body with patience and kindness."

"My mind and body work together in helpful ways."

"I am more than lymphedema."

Now allow yourself to rest quietly in this beautiful garden for a few more moments, knowing that whenever you wish, you can return here in your imagination and once again open the garden gates, one by one, allowing yourself to experience peace, comfort, hope, and healing.

When you are ready, gently bring your awareness back to the room, carrying this feeling of calm with you.

Appendix D

Compression Garment Acceptance Script

Take a slow breath in…
and gently breathe out.

Allow your body to begin settling into a comfortable, relaxed state.

With each breath, your shoulders soften…
your arms rest comfortably…
and your mind becomes a little quieter.

Living with lymphedema can sometimes bring mixed feelings.
You may appreciate the help your treatment provides…
and at the same time wish things were different.

Those feelings are completely understandable.

And right now, as you sit here comfortably, you can begin to explore a new way of thinking about the compression garment that supports your body.

For a moment, imagine that the garment you wear is not a restriction…
but a **supportive partner** working with your body.

Almost like a gentle helper.

You might imagine it as a soft, steady embrace…
providing just the right amount of guidance and support.

Not forcing anything…
simply helping the lymph fluid move comfortably along the pathways designed for it.

In a way, the garment is like a **guide**, gently encouraging the natural flow your body is already trying to create.

And as you imagine this, you might begin to notice a small shift in how it feels.

Instead of something you *have to* wear…
it can become something that **helps you**.

Something that supports your health…
your comfort…
and your ability to move through your day more easily.

You may even imagine thanking your body for all the ways it continues to work for you every day.

And thanking this simple tool—the compression garment—for the role it plays in helping your body maintain balance.

You don't have to force this feeling.

Just allow the idea to gently settle in your mind.

And over time, you may find it becoming easier and more natural to wear the garment…
to see it as something that supports you…
something that helps you take care of yourself.

Because each time you put it on, you are doing something positive for your body.

Something kind.

Something supportive.

And your mind and body can work together in this simple act of self-care.

Take another slow breath in…
and as you breathe out, allow that feeling of cooperation and acceptance to settle comfortably within you.

Self Hypnosis reinforcement.

- *Wearing my garment is an act of caring for my body.*
- *This support helps my body function more comfortably.*
- *I feel calm, confident, and comfortable taking care of my health.*

Appendix E

Coping with Fear, Uncertainty, and the "What Ifs"

Begin this exercise after completing the Progressive Relaxation script.

As you continue to relax, allow yourself to settle even more deeply into this peaceful state. There is nowhere you need to be and nothing you need to do except give yourself this time to rest, restore, and heal.

With every comfortable breath, your body becomes more relaxed, and your mind becomes quieter. As your body relaxes, your thoughts can begin to slow, like gentle ripples on a calm lake gradually becoming still.

Now imagine yourself walking along a peaceful path on a beautiful spring morning. The air is fresh and comfortable. You notice the warmth of the sun on your face, hear birds singing in the distance, and feel a gentle breeze brushing against your skin. Each step you take allows you to feel calmer, lighter, and more at peace.

As you continue walking, you notice that some of your worries have been following you. They are not frightening. They are simply thoughts—the familiar "what ifs" that sometimes appear after a cancer diagnosis.

"What if the cancer comes back?"

"What if they find something?"

"What if this ache means something?"

For a moment, simply notice these thoughts without judging them. They are understandable. They developed because your mind has been trying to protect you after everything you have experienced.

Quietly thank your mind for trying to keep you safe.

Then gently remind yourself:

"Thank you for trying to protect me. Right now, I am safe. I do not need to solve tomorrow's problems today."

As you continue walking, you come to a small stream flowing gently beside the path. Nearby is a basket filled with smooth leaves.

Pick up one leaf.

Place one worry onto that leaf.

Perhaps it is fear of a scan.

Perhaps it is fear of recurrence.

Perhaps it is uncertainty about the future.

Place only one worry on the leaf.

Now gently set the leaf onto the water.

Watch as it slowly drifts downstream.

You do not have to force it away.

You do not have to chase it.

Simply watch it float farther and farther away until it disappears around a bend.

If another worry appears, place it on another leaf.

Allow that one to drift away as well.

One by one, each worry moves downstream, leaving your mind feeling quieter and more peaceful.

Now continue walking until you arrive at a beautiful garden.

The flowers are blooming in every color imaginable.

You notice something remarkable.

Not every flower blooms at exactly the same time.

Some have just opened.

Some are still growing.

Some will bloom later.

Yet every flower unfolds in its own perfect season.

You realize your healing is much the same.

Healing is not a race.

Healing happens one day at a time.

One breath at a time.

One hopeful choice at a time.

As you sit quietly in the garden, notice a beautiful rainbow stretching across the sky.

Allow yourself to take in its colors.

The rainbow reminds you that storms eventually pass.

The storm may have changed you, but it has not taken away your ability to experience hope, joy, love, and peace.

The rainbow reminds you that uncertainty is part of life for everyone.

You do not need certainty to live fully.

You only need this moment.

Allow these thoughts to become part of you now.

I am stronger than I sometimes realize.

I have already overcome challenges I once thought impossible.

I can handle whatever today brings.

I trust myself.

I trust my healthcare team.

I choose to live today rather than fear tomorrow.

Every breath brings greater peace.

Every day I become more confident.

Hope grows stronger within me.

Take a few moments now to imagine yourself at your next medical appointment.

See yourself walking into the office feeling calm and confident.

Notice yourself smiling as you greet the staff.

Feel yourself sitting comfortably while waiting.

Imagine listening carefully to your healthcare provider with a clear, peaceful mind.

Whatever information you receive, know that you will handle it one step at a time, just as you have handled every challenge before.

You leave the appointment feeling proud of yourself—not because you controlled the outcome, but because you chose calm instead of panic.

You chose hope instead of fear.

You chose to trust yourself.

Take one final look at the rainbow.

Allow it to become your symbol of resilience.

Whenever you notice fear beginning to grow, you can simply close your eyes, picture this rainbow, take three slow breaths, and immediately reconnect with the calm, confidence, and strength you are feeling right now.

Know that uncertainty may visit from time to time, but it does not define you.

Fear may occasionally ride beside you, but it no longer drives your life.

Hope is now your companion.

Strength is within you.

Peace is available to you.

And each new day offers another opportunity to discover the rainbow after the storm.

When you are ready, allow yourself to return to full awareness, bringing back with you a renewed sense of calm, confidence, hope, and peace...feeling refreshed, relaxed, and ready to enjoy the rest of your day.

Appendix F

The Control Room Technique

One of the most effective self-hypnosis methods for managing discomfort is the **Control Room Technique**, which helps patients imagine themselves adjusting the intensity of pain in much the same way they would adjust the volume on a television or radio.

After guiding yourself into a comfortable hypnotic state, imagine walking into a beautiful control room created entirely by your own mind. The room contains everything needed to control the sensations in your body.

In front of you is a large control panel with a clearly marked dial labeled **Comfort** and another labeled **Discomfort**. A digital screen displays the current level of discomfort on a scale from **0 to 10**.

Observe the number without judgment—simply noticing where it is at that moment.

Gently place your hand on the Comfort Control.

As you slowly turn the dial upward, imagine feelings of warmth, relaxation, numbness, or soothing comfort spreading throughout your body, especially where the discomfort is at the moment.

At the same time, you gradually turn the Discomfort Control downward.

Watch the number on the screen slowly decrease—from perhaps an 8...to a 7...to a 6...and continuing downward to whatever level feels realistic and comfortable for you.

With every adjustment, you notice your muscles becoming looser, your breathing slower, and your body feeling lighter and more at ease.

Remember, you remain in complete control. You can return to this control room whenever you wish—anytime discomfort becomes noticeable.

With practice, simply closing your eyes, taking a few slow breaths, and imagining yourself entering your control room would quickly activate the same feelings of comfort and relaxation, allowing you to reduce discomfort and regain a greater sense of control over your body.

Resources for Patients, Survivors, and Caregivers

No one should have to face cancer alone. The following organizations offer reliable, up-to-date information, educational materials, emotional support, financial assistance, and practical resources for patients, survivors, and caregivers. While treatments and recommendations continue to evolve, these organizations are trusted sources of information.

American Cancer Society (ACS)

Website: https://www.cancer.org
Phone: 1-800-227-2345

The American Cancer Society provides comprehensive information about all types of cancer, treatment options, side effects, survivorship, transportation assistance, lodging programs, support services, and caregiver resources. Their trained cancer information specialists are available 24 hours a day.

National Cancer Institute (NCI)

Website: https://www.cancer.gov
Phone: 1-800-4-CANCER (1-800-422-6237)

The National Cancer Institute is the federal government's principal agency for cancer research. Their website offers evidence-based information on diagnosis, treatment, clinical trials, coping, survivorship, and cancer prevention, along with easy-to-understand educational materials.

CancerCare

Website: https://www.cancercare.org
Phone: 1-800-813-HOPE (4673)

CancerCare provides free counseling by oncology social workers, educational workshops, online and telephone support groups, resource navigation, and limited financial assistance for eligible patients.

LIVESTRONG Foundation

Website: https://www.livestrong.org

LIVESTRONG offers practical guidance for people living with cancer, including survivorship resources, fertility information, financial guidance, caregiver support, and healthy living after treatment.

National Comprehensive Cancer Network (NCCN) – Patient Guidelines

Website: https://www.nccn.org/patientresources

NCCN provides free, evidence-based patient guidelines that explain many cancer diagnoses and treatments in language that is easier to understand than medical textbooks. These guides can help patients prepare questions for their healthcare team.

Local Cancer Centers and Hospitals

Many hospitals and cancer centers offer:

- Support groups
- Nutrition counseling
- Oncology social workers
- Financial counselors
- Rehabilitation services

- Exercise programs
- Integrative medicine
- Survivorship programs

Ask your oncology team what services are available in your community.

Your Healthcare Team

Never hesitate to ask questions. Your oncologist, surgeon, radiation oncologist, oncology nurses, social workers, dietitians, physical therapists, and other healthcare professionals are important members of your care team. They want you to understand your diagnosis and participate in decisions about your care.

Remember...

The internet contains an overwhelming amount of information—some excellent, some misleading, and some simply incorrect. Whenever possible, rely on reputable organizations and discuss any questions or concerns with your healthcare providers before making changes to your treatment or healthcare plan.

Most importantly, remember that you are not alone. Help, hope, and support are available every step of the way.

Resources Hypnosis-Friendly Cancer Support Programs

These programs specifically include hypnosis, hypnotherapy, guided imagery, self-hypnosis, or hypno-oncology approaches as part of cancer support.

Hypno-Oncology International

A professional network of accredited hypno-oncology practitioners supporting people through the cancer journey. They emphasize that hypnosis is an adjunctive emotional-support therapy, not a cancer treatment. Support may include anxiety reduction, coping with treatment side effects, fear management, relaxation, and emotional resilience.

Hypnoncology – Hypnocell®

Offers hypnosis-based mind-body programs specifically designed for cancer patients. Focuses on guided imagery, relaxation, subconscious support work, and emotional healing alongside conventional medical care.

VCU Massey Comprehensive Cancer Center Integrative Medicine – Hypnosis

A major cancer center offering hypnosis within integrative oncology services. Often used to support stress reduction, pain management, nausea control, and treatment-related anxiety.

Stanford Health Care – Cancer and Hypnosis

Stanford's integrative medicine program discusses the role of hypnosis in helping cancer patients manage pain, fear, anxiety, stress, and depression during treatment.

CASSI – Cancer Symptom Science Interventions (University of Tennessee)

Research-based program studying self-hypnosis and other behavioral interventions for cancer-related symptoms such as insomnia, hot flashes, fatigue, and cognitive symptoms in survivors.

Honest Courage Cancer Coaching & Hypno-Oncology

Provides cancer-focused hypnotherapy, RTT®, group coaching, and emotional support programs for patients, survivors, and caregivers. Also hosts "Cancer Salon" support gatherings.

New ECaP – New Exceptional Cancer Patients

A free online mindfulness-based cancer support group influenced by the work of Bernie Siegel. Combines emotional support, mindfulness, guided imagery, and community connection.

Mind-Body & Integrative Cancer Support Programs

These programs focus on emotional healing, meditation, yoga, guided imagery, expressive arts, resilience training, and integrative oncology.

Unite for HER

National nonprofit providing free integrative wellness therapies and support for breast and ovarian cancer patients. Includes meditation, nutrition, acupuncture, yoga, counseling, wellness education, and community support.

Beat the Odds – Mind-Body Oncology Program

A comprehensive mind-body oncology program focused on stress reduction, emotional resilience, guided imagery, group support, and psycho-oncology approaches for patients and families.

UCSF Meditation & Guided Imagery for Cancer Patients

Free online meditation and guided imagery classes through the UCSF Osher Center for Integrative Health and UCSF Cancer Support Center.

UC San Diego Moores Cancer Center – Mind & Body Wellness Classes

Virtual wellness classes including expressive arts, relaxation practices, mindfulness, resilience support, and supportive community programming for cancer patients and caregivers.

Mount Sinai Tisch Cancer Center Support Services

Offers comprehensive psychosocial and supportive oncology services including counseling, peer mentorship, spiritual care, stress management, and wellness support.

About the Author

Joann Abrahamsen has spent more than three decades helping people create meaningful and lasting change through the power of hypnosis. A board-certified consultant in hypnosis through both the National Guild of Hypnotists (NGH) and the International Certification Board of Coaches and Hypnotists (ICBCH), she is an internationally recognized keynote speaker, educator, author, and certified consultant in hypnosis.

Throughout her career, Joann has been honored for her contributions to the hypnosis profession. She was inducted into the National Guild of Hypnotists' Order of Braid, recognizing a lifetime of outstanding achievement, dedication, and service, and is the recipient of the National Guild of Hypnotists' Charles Tebbetts Award, the Outstanding Achievement Award, and the Association to Advance Ethical Hypnosis' Person of the Year Award, as well as the President's Award and the Harry Arons Award. She was also inducted into the Hypnosis Hall of Fame.

Joann is a certified instructor for both the NGH and the ICBCH and teaches hypnosis certification courses both online and in person. She is a frequent presenter for national and international hypnosis organizations and has taught hypnosis courses for adults through local schools and colleges. In her private practice, she combines award-winning hypnotic techniques with practical behavior modification to help clients overcome challenges and achieve their personal goals.

A regular columnist for the *Journal of Hypnotism*, Joann was featured on the cover of its March 2022 issue. She is also certified in Neuro-Linguistic Programming (NLP) and Life Coaching by the ICBCH and has been voted "Best of Yonkers" for hypnosis services for three consecutive years.

Joann is the author of *The Rainbow after the Storm: Surviving and Thriving After a Cancer Diagnosis*, *Weighing in on Hypnosis: Lifestyle and Habit Changes for Weight Loss Success*, *Self-Hypnosis: Easy as 1, 2, 3*, and *A Potpourri of Hypnotic Techniques.*

When she is not writing, teaching, or working with clients, Joann enjoys ballroom dancing, line dancing, singing karaoke with her husband, Robert Fried, and traveling with him—especially cruising. They live in Westchester County, New York, with their delightful calico cat, Nutmeg.

For information about Joann's books, speaking engagements, hypnosis services, certification training, or to contact her directly, please see her contact page

CANCER BELL INSCRIPTION

RING THIS BELL
THREE TIMES WELL
TO CELEBRATE THIS DAY!

THIS COURSE IS RUN,
MY TREATMENT DONE,
NOW I AM ON MY WAY!

Before You Close This Book

Before you turn this final page, I invite you to pause for a moment and look again at the photograph of me ringing the cancer bell.

For many cancer patients, the ringing of the bell marks the completion of treatment. For me, on December 21, 2020, it represented much more. It was a moment of gratitude, relief, hope, and the realization that although my treatments had ended, a new journey was just beginning—the journey of survivorship.

If this book has found its way into your hands, I hope it has reminded you that a cancer diagnosis is not the end of your story. It may change the path you are traveling, but it does not have to define who you are or take away your hope for the future.

It has been my privilege to share my journey with you, along with the stories and wisdom of other survivors who so generously opened their hearts. My hope is that somewhere within these pages you have found encouragement, comfort, practical guidance, and, most importantly, the reassurance that you are never alone.

Throughout this book, I have shared many of the self-hypnosis techniques that helped me through my own cancer journey. If you would like to continue using these techniques, I'm pleased to share that I am preparing a companion workbook that will bring together all of the hypnosis exercises and scripts from this book in one convenient place, along with additional techniques designed to help patients, survivors, and caregivers navigate the emotional and physical challenges of cancer.

The companion workbook is expected to be available in January. If you follow me as an author on Amazon, you'll automatically be notified as soon as it is released.

If you are looking for additional encouragement, self-hypnosis resources, or information about my work with cancer patients, survivors, and caregivers, I invite you to contact me using the information on the About the Author page. It would be my honor to continue walking beside you on your journey.

If this book brought you comfort, offered you hope, or helped you face your own cancer journey with greater confidence, then it has fulfilled the purpose for which it was written.

If this book has touched your life, may I ask one small favor?

If you found this book helpful, I would be deeply grateful if you would consider leaving a brief review on Amazon or wherever you purchased your copy. Your review helps other patients, survivors, caregivers, and families discover this book when they need it most. Your few kind words may provide hope to someone who is just beginning one of the most difficult journeys of their life.

I leave you with one final thought:

Never stop looking for your rainbow.

Even after the darkest storms, it is still possible to find hope, healing, joy, laughter, and beauty again. No matter where you are on your journey today, may you move forward with courage, strength, peace, and the confidence that brighter days are still ahead.

Thank you for allowing me to share my story—and for trusting me to become a small part of yours.

With gratitude, hope, and my very best wishes,

Joann Abrahamsen

May you always find your rainbow after the storm.

www.ingramcontent.com/pod-product-compliance
Lightning Source LLC
LaVergne TN
LVHW052318200926
848481LV00002B/601
* 9 7 9 8 9 8 6 6 5 3 1 3 6 *